DRYBU ABBEY

the late **J S Richardson**
formerly *Inspector of Ancient Monuments for Scotland*

with revisions by
C J Tabraham
Principal Inspector of Ancient Monuments

HISTORIC SCOTLAND

EDINBURGH: HMSO

1

2

'A ruin of great charm'

The abbey of Dryburgh is situated beside a most picturesque stretch of the River Tweed, between the burghs of Melrose and Kelso. Here, on a sheltered tongue of pleasing, fertile ground, the White Canons of the Premonstratensian Order established their first home on Scottish soil in 1150. Though the monastery never quite aspired to the heights of wealth and political influence enjoyed by the neighbouring Border abbeys of Jedburgh, Kelso and Melrose, it proved nonetheless their equal as a source of attraction to the many English raiding parties that bedevilled Border life for some three centuries. Devastated by fire in 1322, 1385, 1461 and again in 1523, the monastery never recovered from the ravages of Hertford's army in the 1540s, and the last canon died before that century was out. Today, Dryburgh is perhaps best remembered as the burial place of Sir Walter Scott.

This guide-book contains a short tour (pages 4–5), extended tour (pages 7–21) and history of Dryburgh Abbey (pages 23–31), together with a glossary (page 32).

A view of the south transept of Dryburgh Abbey from a drawing by W H Lizars in 1831.

3

'An ordered life'

G o through the west doorway (bottom left on plan) into the **nave** of the abbey church, largely rebuilt in the fifteenth century following repeated devastations by English raiding parties. Here laypeople from the district were allowed to attend church services.

Walk towards the **choir**, reserved for the canons (regular monks) and novices (new admissions), who were required to attend a

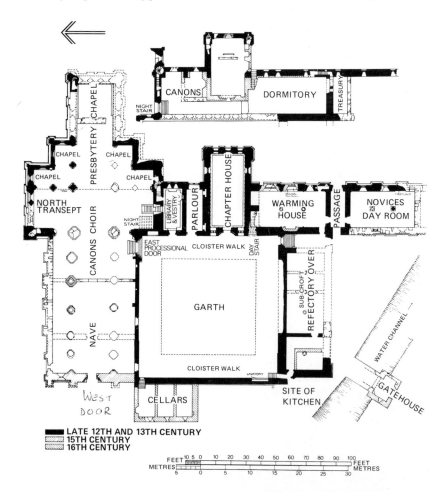

LATE 12TH AND 13TH CENTURY
15TH CENTURY
16TH CENTURY

total of eight services during the course of a 24-hour day. They were seated in carved wooden stalls (novices in front, canons to the rear) set against the pillars supporting the arcading. The high altar was set against the screen at the east end of the **presbytery**. Subsidiary altars were placed in numerous **chapels** in the north and south transepts where masses were said for the souls of benefactors of the monastery. These chapels were subsequently appropriated by notable families of the district for private burial places.

Ascend the night-stair in the south transept and enter the **dormitory**. Originally a single chamber, with canons sleeping next to the church and the novices in the (now unfloored) remainder to the south, it was altered after the Reformation to provide accommodation for the commendator (lay administrator).

Descend the night-stair and pass through the doorway into the **cloister**, around which were grouped the conventual buildings, the business and domestic apartments of the community. The cloister walk was formerly covered by a lean-to roof falling from the walls of the surrounding buildings to an open arcade looking into the **garth**, perhaps laid out in vegetable beds or as a herb garden, not grass as today. The four covered walks served as areas of private contemplation or study in addition to affording sheltered passages.

Walk along the east walk and observe, in turn, the **library** and **vestry** (since appropriated by David Stuart, earl of Buchan for his burial place), **parlour**, where the only conversation was permitted (since appropriated by the Erskines for their burial place), **chapter-house**, the administrative and business centre of the abbey, and **day-stair**, affording day-time access from dormitory to cloister and church.

Descend the flight of steps at the end and view the **warming-house**, the only chamber, other than the kitchen, novices' day-room and infirmary, where a fireplace was permitted, **passage**, giving access to the monastic cemetery and **infirmary**, or hospital, beyond and **novices' day-room**, within which the master of the novices gave instruction to the new admissions.

Pass along the south range, noting the remains of the **subcroft**, where provisions were stored which, when prepared in the kitchen (now since demolished), were consumed in the **refectory** (dining-hall) above. The brethren were permitted only one main meal each day—dinner (*Prandium*) at midday—with perhaps a light breakfast (*Mixtum*) and supper (*Caena*).

Cross the channel, bringing fresh running water from the River Tweed, and view the ruined **gatehouse** built after the Reformation.

Recross the channel and ascend the flight of steps to the west walk. On your left is the **lavatory**, wash-basins where the brethren rinsed their hands before mealtimes. At the north (far) end, go through the doorway into three vaulted **cellars**, built after the Reformation and now housing a collection of stonework. Re-enter the cloister, pass along the north walk and return to the church.

Opposite page: Ground plan of the surviving abbey buildings.

The abbey as it may have appeared in the fifteenth century. A reconstruction by the late Alan Sorrell.

Church and Cloister

Plan

Dryburgh was selected in 1150 by the Canons Regular of the Premonstratensian Order for their first home in Scotland. The White Canons set out their abbey on lines similar to that of the parent house at Alnwick, Northumberland. This made provision for an aisled cruciform church 57 m long; a cloister 27 m square; a long eastern range containing vestry, parlour, chapter-house, day-stair, warming-house, passage and novices' room, with the canons' and novices' dormitories on the first floor; a southern range comprising passage, refectory with subcroft and kitchen. A high wall enclosed the cloister instead of the usual western range found at other monastic buildings. Owing to the site being on a slope, the buildings at Dryburgh were erected on three prepared stepped levels. From the highest of these the abbey church, the largest and loftiest of the group, overlooked the cloister, which is on the next or middle level. On the lowest level stood the chapter-house, the principal day apartments, the cellars and the kitchen. This stepped arrangement and the shelter of the surrounding buildings gave to the cloister all the advantages of a sunny exposure.

The original layout was bounded on the north by a precinct wall and included the infirmary, abbot's lodging, guest-house, bakehouse and brew-house, mill, barns, orchard and yards, but there is now no trace of any of these.

Temporary structures of wood served to house the community for some time during the preparation of their permanent home. It is probable that the masons who worked at the abbey of Alnwick were employed at Dryburgh.

Building materials

Building material was obtained from freestone quarries situated to the north of the abbey and also on the opposite bank of the river; there the ashlar and the moulded details were prepared. This Dryburgh stone, which has a beautiful, clean, warm and mellow tint, gives great charm to the appearance of the ruined abbey. The oak beams required for roofing and the timber for the construction of the buildings were obtained in the immediate vicinity. Lime came from near Kelso.

The abbey church

The original church was dedicated to St Mary. Very little of it remains but its scale and proportions can be judged by the ruined north and south transepts and the low walls and pillars which indicate the plan. At the crossing a square bell-tower rose above the level of the steeply pitched roof of the main body of the building.

Judging by the number and size of the remaining windows, St Mary's was unusually well lighted for a church of its period. Owing to the low level of the cloister, the south aisle of the nave obtained direct lighting from above the roof of the cloister walk. The clerestory windows (those above the level of the aisle roofs) were connected by a mural passage which led round the church giving access for the care and maintenance of the glass. From the clerestory passage outside covered steps led down to the gallery, which is the space under the roof and over the stone vault of the aisles. The clerestory passage was reached from the ground level by three narrow wheel-stairs, within the two transepts and the presbytery.

West front

The western half of the church was reconstructed after the extensive damage wrought by the English in 1385.

The entrance to the church is in the middle of the west front. This fifteenth-century doorway is round-headed, heavily moulded and enriched by carved blocks, each ornamented with a design of four conventional leaves. Unfortunately the surrounding face-stones have been removed. A large window of flowing tracery occupied a position over the entrance and fragments of the tracery are in the small collection of carved and moulded details arranged in the cellars entered from the north-west corner of the cloister.

Nave

The nave had north and south vaulted aisles and was divided into six bays. The north wall is reduced to the level of the basement course, and little is left of the pillars that supported the arcading. The evidence indicating the construction of this end of the church is to be seen where the north arcade joined the west wall. The main roofing of the nave, the transepts and presbytery, was of timber set at a steep pitch. Under the tower the crossing was ceiled with a rib-and-panel vault.

Scratched onto a foundation stone in the ruined north wall of the nave (and now marked off by a small wire enclosure) is a merelles board. The board game of merelles was introduced into England by the Normans but there are only four known

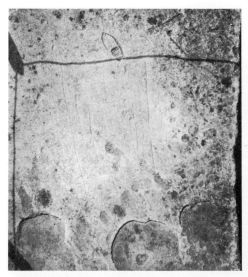

The merelles board.

8

A view through the fifteenth-century west door of the abbey church looking towards the ruined north transept.

examples in Scotland. All appear to be of thirteenth-century date and it may be that the Dryburgh board was scratched by stonemasons working on the construction of the abbey. The game is similar to modern 'noughts and crosses'.

Choir

The choir, containing the canons' stalls, was separated from the nave by a screen, or *pulpitum*, which stretched across the church in line with the pillars situated two bays west of the crossing. The foundation of this screen remains with the threshold of its doorway in the centre. In the aisles of the nave and also the aisles of the first bay east of the *pulpitum* were chapels housing side altars. In the south aisle south chapels there are mural *piscinae* or sinks, where the vessels used at mass were washed. Above the level of these features the wall has been rebuilt and to the east of the west cloister doorway there is indication of a pause in the work of the building. The walls of the church are buttressed externally with the exception of the south wall of the nave which has internal responds.

Transepts

The transepts project a bay's width beyond the lateral walls of the nave. Each has two eastern chapels; the inner chapels, two bays deep, line with the nave aisles and had arcades opening into the presbytery. The building of the transepts and the eastern end of the church was commenced at the same time, as shown by the basement course on the outside. Slight differences in the upper architectural treatment indicate interruptions in the building operations, or the influence of fresh ideas.

The original appearance of the eastern half of the church is best illustrated by the remains of the north transept and its eastern chapels. The less-ruined state of this part of the building is no doubt due to the fact that it did not suffer complete destruction at the time when the tower collapsed, and also to the fact that the chapels had been appropriated by notable families of the district for their burial places. Principal among these were the Haliburtons, whose most distinguished representative, Sir Walter Scott, is interred here. The details and

The canons' choir with, beyond, the north transept (left), the presbytery (now largely disappeared) and the south transept (right). The great window in the south transept lit the canons' dormitory.

10

The north window in the north choir chapel, with its dog-tooth decoration to the hood mould and the flanking nook shafts (now missing). The quality of the original masonry is clearly apparent.

The surviving lancet window of the triplet of windows which originally pierced the lower level of the north transept gable. The combination of continuous and supported arch mouldings is particularly pleasing.

mouldings inside the building exhibit the same quality of workmanship and design as those on the outside, and the high standard of the mason's craft is to be seen in the carefully undercut dog-tooth enrichments on the moulded labels. The carvings were cut before they were built into position. This is best observed where a carved human head, as in the case of the bat carving, is so placed that it was necessary to make an indent in the wall for the display of the ornament.

The north gable had two storeys of triple lancets, moulded and enriched with the same design on both sides. Probably there was a window in the upper part of the gable. The buttress at the north-west angle accommodated a wheel-stair.

The eastern chapels each contained an altar and are ceiled with rib-and-panel vaulting of a later type than that in the warming-house and novices' day-room. The ribs are moulded and at the intersections there are carved massive keystones or bosses, one of which represents Christ in Majesty holding a book in the left hand, while the right hand is raised in blessing. On some of the vault ribs there

are traces of mural decoration in red on a white ground and fragments are also to be seen on the east wall near the window. The north chapel is provided with a *piscina* in the east wall.

The gallery over the vaults was cramped in area but was made use of by the community. It has windows at the gable ends and cusped circular lights opening into the church. The entrance was from the clerestory passage. The clerestory arcade exhibits slight differences in style and this is apparent on the north wall of the presbytery. On the outside face of the north transept there are marks caused by bullets, possibly made when the abbey suffered at the hands of the 'auld enemy' in 1544.

Presbytery
The presbytery, containing the high altar, occupied the narrowest part of the church. There is little to indicate its original appearance for the existing portion has been robbed of its face work. Each of the side walls had three lancet windows; the remains of one

The presbytery and north transept from the north-east. In the foreground the chapels opening off the north transept and choir are to be seen, with the clerestory windows which lit the central spaces rising above them. In the left foreground are the lower walls of the presbytery, behind which is the gable wall of the south transept.

of these is to be seen in the north wall. The east wall had an architectural treatment similar to that of the north wall of the transept. The clerestory arrangement of the transepts was continued above the windows on the side walls. Inside the building under the windows there was a wall arcading composed of short pillars and semi-circular intersecting arches. This feature, rising from a shallow stone bench, resembles the arcading in the chapter-house and it appears to have been altered. It was afterwards disfigured before the final destruction of the church.

An exposed foundation in the presbytery may have carried a screen behind the high altar; a similar feature was noted by the excavators of the ruins of the abbey church at Alnwick. If there was a screen, then there must have been a chapel beyond.

The night-stair, at the south-west corner of the south transept, led to the canons' dormitory and was used by the canons for their attendance at the night services. Beside the stair is a doorway leading to the vestry which is at a lower level. This entrance was altered in post-Reformation times. Opening from the corner chapel is a narrow round-headed doorway leading to the bell-stair which served to connect the vestry, the dormitory, the clerestory and the roof. On the east wall within the doorway is a holy water stoup.

The pointed window in the west wall over the night-stair has an internal label terminating in two carved corbels representing bat-like animals clinging to the wall. The one in the corner gives the impression of peering into a cavity purposely cut in the wall. Over the window is a section

The south transept. The stair (known as the night-stair) afforded the monks a link between their dormitory and the choir of the church for the night services without them having to walk out into the open air. To the right is the entrance to the cloisters.

13

of the clerestory passage which leads to a doorway giving access to the roof of the eastern range, and passes under the great window in the upper part of the transept gable. This window is slightly pointed and has a stepped sill, so designed to accommodate the abutting roof over the canons' dormitory. The infilling of the windows is of simple geometric design and is composed of five lancets and four spandrel openings. Originally it was glazed throughout; later the lower part was built up and finally the entire window was blocked with masonry which was removed at the commencement of the nineteenth century.

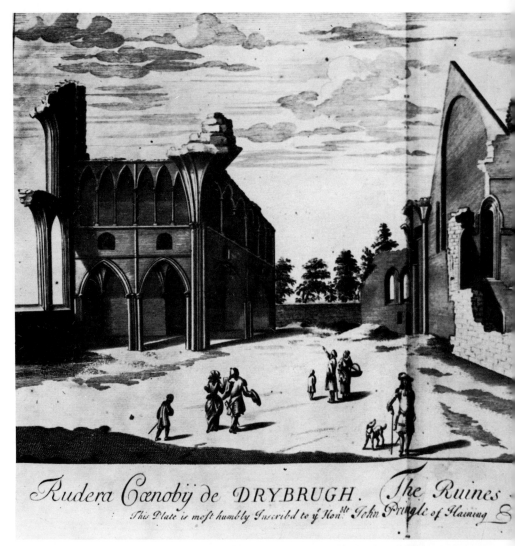

Rudera Cænobij de DRYBRUGH. The Ruines
This Plate is most humbly Inscribd to y Honble John Pringle of Haining

The abbey ruins sketched from the west door by Captain John Slezer in 1678. The east end of the church (on the left) has altered little since that time. The east range of the cloister (on the right) has, in the interval, lost the fine range of windows lighting the monks' dormitory at first floor level (see photograph on page 13 for a comparison).

THE CONVENTUAL BUILDINGS

Dormitory

The dormitory, which originally extended the entire length of the first floor of the east range, is entered via the night-stair in the south transept. The regular canons occupied the part nearest the church, the novices the remainder away to the south. A range of

the Abbey of DRYBRUGH

round-headed windows along the west wall afforded the monks a view across their cloister.

There was also a small stair in the east wall connecting the part of the dormitory used by the novices with a narrow vaulted room over the vaulted passage and lying at an intermediate level between the ground and the first floor.

The outline of the original timber roof over the dormitory can be seen under the great window where it abutted on the wall of the south transept. There is evidence of the destruction of the roof by fire. In the subsequent reconstruction the part of the building overlooking the cloister was carried up to the height of the south transept, an unusual arrangement. This addition provided extra accommodation, and is shown in Slezer's engraving of the abbey (c 1678). The dormitory wall over the north end of the warming-house also suffered in the fire; it was strengthened by widening on the inside, and when this was done the openings of the round-headed windows were curtailed. In the sixteenth century alterations were made to the dormitory immediately over the chapter-house to make it suitable for the commendator's house. Dwelling rooms were constructed, large square-headed windows were introduced at the eastern end and a new access formed from the east side.

The latrine-block or *reredorter* was entered off the dormitory and contained a water-flushed pit. This building has not been found, but it probably projected beyond the south end of the eastern range.

Cloister

The cloister, which comprised the business and domestic apartments, has had three entrances from the church. The east processional doorway is the one now in use. The facade of the doorway faces the cloister and has an arched semi-circular head, moulded and enriched with dog-tooth ornament. The splayed sides have recessed 'orders' with disengaged shafts and the caps on the east side are plain but those on the west are carved with foliaceous ornament. This doorway, which had been removed to the mansion of Newton Don, near Kelso, was restored to the abbey by Capt C B Balfour, CB, in 1894.

The square open space known as the cloister garth was surrounded by a covered walk; on the garth side was an open arcaded wall, the foundations of which have been traced. A few corbels and fragmentary bands of water-tabling on the main walls are evidence of the lean-to roof of the cloister walk.

Library and vestry

Vault-rib springers indicate that the east walk was vaulted in the thirteenth century. Near the processional doorway is a wall-press, or aumbry, once fitted with doors and shelves to contain the books used in the cloister. Several chambers open off the walk. The first of these, a barrel-vaulted chamber now known as 'St Modan's Chapel', is furnished with stone benches. This chamber served as a library and vestry. Besides the entrance from the cloister it has two doorways, one leading

The east processional doorway linking church and cloister.

up a flight of steps to the south transept, the other by way of a wheel-stair to a transept chapel and to the higher levels of the building. The vestry is lighted by three windows in the east wall; the uppermost is almond-shaped and is an insertion of slightly later date. The pavement is raised at the east end and contains a *piscina* which was probably transferred from the floor of the church. There is also a *piscina* in the south wall. Traces of colour decoration in red, blue and black lines are to be noted on the projecting impost from which the barrel vault springs. David Stuart, earl of Buchan, bought the abbey of Dryburgh in 1730 and appropriated this chamber for his burial place. The earl carried out works of

The cloister with the church behind. The cloister was used by the monks for private devotion and contemplation. The largest of the doorways in this east range led into the chapter-house, the main administrative area. The doorway on the far right afforded access to a stair (the day-stair) leading to the dormitory on the floor above.

preservation on the ruin but unfortunately was responsible for introducing certain misleading features as, for instance, the carved memorial pillar standing in the grounds to the south of the gate-house, and probably the 'Hic jacet Archibaldus' inscription cut on the wall beside the entrance to the chapter-house. He was one of the founders of the Society of Antiquaries of Scotland in 1780.

Parlour
The second doorway in the cloister leads into the parlour, the only place throughout the abbey where the canons were permitted to converse. It is barrel-vaulted and the benches which flanked the walls must have been of wood since there is no evidence of their having been of stone. In the south wall are two mural aumbries. The parlour served as a processional passage from the cloister to the canons' cemetery. At the beginning of the nineteenth century this passage was used as a burial place by the Erskine family. The doorway from the cloister was curtailed and the other was walled up and a window was introduced.

Chapter-house

The third doorway leads to the chapter-house and resembles in its architectural treatment the east processional doorway; it is flanked by two open arcades. A flight of steps leads down to the floor, some 1.5 m below the level of the cloister walk. The chapter-house has a barrel-vault and the windows are grouped at the east end, which projects beyond the line of the outer wall of the eastern range. There are stone benches for the canons on all sides. Over the bench at the east end is a wall arcade in stone of semi-circular intersecting arches carried on shafts, a design which was repeated in colour round the other walls. Here the abbot and his senior officers sat and conducted their business. There is evidence to suggest that the lower part of the arcade was draped with hangings. On the east wall the upper part of the arcading has been decorated with painted geometric patterns. Fragments of mural paintings remain on the groin of the vaulting of the north window. The chapter-house was used daily by the community for the reading of a chapter from the Rule of the Order, hence its name.

Preserved within the chapter-house is a rectangular basin of freestone carved in relief on all four sides with bird-like creatures with intertwined necks and tails, the latter terminating in floral display. It may have formed part of an older wash-basin. It was found over a hundred years ago near the refectory entrance; part of the lead overflow pipe was then still attached to it (see back cover).

Day-stair

The next opening from the cloister is the entrance to the day-stair (now ruined) which was used by the canons for access to their dormitory during the day. The stair was radically altered in the sixteenth century when the commendator's house was erected in the dormitory on the first floor; steps branched off and led to the ground on the outside of the building.

At the south-east corner of the cloister a

In the twelfth and thirteenth centuries monastic chapter-houses characteristically had their entrances flanked by twin-light windows. This, the right-hand window of the pair, has capitals of the type usually likened to chalices.

stairway and passage, originally barrel-vaulted, lead down to the lowest floor levels, and to the vaulted through-passage of the eastern range. A doorway on the north side of this passage gives access to the warming-house; another on the south side leads to the novices' day-room.

Warming-house

The warming-house, or calefactory, the chamber in which the canons were allowed the comfort of a fire, had a central line of pillars and was vaulted in six compartments. The caps that support the vault ribs are of slender treatment and have pronounced projections. In the fourteenth century a hooded fireplace was built in the centre of the west wall; its corbels are carved with leaf patterns, one depicting oak leaves with acorns. The original fireplace was in the east wall. It was removed in order to introduce two pointed arch-headed windows for the improvement of the lighting of the room. At the south-east corner is a small mural closet

The interior of the chapter-house. Here the abbot, who would be seated on the bench in the centre of the far wall, and his brethren conducted their business affairs. The chapter-house at Dryburgh is one of few which has remains of wall painting.

A close-up of a wall painting within one of the semi-circular intersecting arches at the east end of the chapter-house.

and close to it there was a doorway leading to the outside. This doorway and a small round-headed window above it are alterations. In the eighteenth-century the warming-house was used as a cow byre and the vaults were then intact.

Novices' day-room

The novices' day-room resembles the warming-house, but the fireplace is in the original position in the east wall and the windows have not been altered. The pattern carved on the outside of the windows is similar to the ornament used on the doorway in the south transept chapel.

Refectory and subcroft

The building on the south side of the cloister at the lowest ground level contained a subcroft of two vaulted apartments with central pillars. The windows were in the south wall. In the fifteenth century the rooms were reconstructed as barrel-vaulted cellars and a passage was formed. On the walls of the passage can be seen rows of small incised crosses, possibly the tallies cut by a cellarer.

Above this basement was the refectory (dining-hall) approached by a flight of steps from the cloister walk. The dais, or raised platform where the high table stood, was at the east end and close to it, on the south wall, was a pulpit for the reader at meals. The refectory was lighted by four large windows in the south wall, small windows in the north wall and the wheel, or rose, window in the west gable which still remains intact. A screen divided the west end of the hall from the main body; the servery passage from the kitchen entered at this point. The coat-of-arms over the doorway which leads from the cloister walk to the kitchen is a sixteenth-century carving and the arms are those of John Stewart, second son of the earl of Lennox (see page 28).

The outer wall of the east conventual range with the flank of the chapter-house to the right. Several phases of alterations to the original ranks of round-headed windows are clearly evident. The two enlarged Y-traceried windows lit the warming-house.

The refectory (dining-hall). It was lit by windows in the north and south walls and by a wheel, or rose window in the west gable. The rose window (fifteenth-century) is a rare survival, although a similar example can be seen in the west gable of Jedburgh Abbey church. The arched recess on the right is where the monks washed their hands before going to dinner. The gate-house stands to the left.

Gate-house

To the south of the refectory, and on the opposite side of the ditch which was the old water-channel, is a small gate-house. It was at one time connected with the main buildings by a covered bridge but only the lower part of this now remains. The gate-house contained a passage and on the first floor was a small chamber entered from the vaulted top of the bridge. Heraldic shields are carved on the skew-putts of the gables; the one on the west side bears the arms of the Greenlaw family and the other represents the arms of the House of Ker.

Lavatory

An arched recess, the principal feature in the west wall of the cloister, is situated at the corner conveniently near the entrance to the refectory. This recess contained the lead-lined trough for hand-washing before meals, the water being supplied through a conduit. The bench and the masonry at the back of the recess are modern.

Cellars

No provision was apparently made in the original plan for a western range but at a later period three vaulted cellars were constructed against the west wall at the north end. These are entered from the cloister through a plain round-headed doorway. A carved grave-slab has been used as an internal lintel. The cellars now shelter a small collection of moulded and carved stones from different parts of the abbey.

The abbey and grounds from the south-east. Nestling on a tongue
of land beside the River Tweed in its unspoiled rural setting,
Dryburgh is a most attractive monument.

'A peaceful refuge'

The earliest ecclesiastical mention of Dryburgh is somewhat legendary and derives from sources no longer extant. A calendar of Scottish Saints gives for 4 February 'Sanctus Modanus, Abbas Drijburgensis'. The name of St Modan, one of St Columba's followers, is connected with Roseneath, Dunbartonshire, and the eastern Lowlands of Scotland. It has been suggested that he was at Dryburgh about AD 622, using the place as headquarters, whence he went on his missionary journeys to places so far afield as Falkirk, Stirling, Dumfries, Roseneath and Loch Etive in Argyll. But the invasion of the pagan king of Northumbria, sweeping over the Lowlands, effaced any trace, leaving the work of the first Columban missionaries to be recommenced by such men as St Aidan, St Boisil and St Cuthbert from the monastery of Old Melrose.

Foundation

The Chronicle of Melrose records the arrival of the Order of Premonstratensians at Dryburgh on St Martin's Day, 1150, and again that on 12 December 1152, the monastery came to that place. Between these dates we may presume the building and some measure of completion of the abbey and conventual buildings. The first stage in the establishment of the abbey seems to have been the consecration of the cemetery which took place on the day of the arrival of the order. The actual consecration of the church of St Mary of Dryburgh does not seem to be noted.

The Premonstratensians, known also as the White Canons from the colour of their habit, were a comparatively recent order, founded by St Norbert in 1121, following the rule of St Augustine with certain modifications. The name of the order is taken from its first seat, Prémontré, near Laon in France.

The order grew rapidly and eventually there were several hundred monasteries throughout Europe answerable to Prémontré. The first house of the order in England was the abbey of Newhouse, Lincolnshire. From its daughter house of Alnwick, founded in 1140, the White Canons came to Dryburgh. There were five other houses in Scotland: Soulseat (c 1161), Whithorn (c 1175), Tongland (1218) and Holywood (by 1225) in Galloway, and Fearn (c 1225) in Ross.

Abbey lands

The founder, Hugh de Moreville, constable of Scotland, and his wife bestowed on the abbey of Dryburgh endowments, among which were the churches of Borgue, Channelkirk and Saltoun, not only the actual buildings but the lands with which they were endowed. From later information it appears that the canons might either serve the churches themselves, or else appoint a vicar. The constable also bestowed on them a ploughgate of land in Newton which William, his steward, held, stretching from the west of Dere Street—the Roman road—to the bound of Thirlestane, together with pasturage for four oxen and a horse. His wife, Beatrix de Bello Campo, granted the church of Bozeat in Northamptonshire. The administration of the gift proved difficult at so great a distance and about 1190 the monastery came to an agreement with the abbey of St James at Northampton. To that place Helen de Moreville had granted land in Lauder. An exchange was made. Dryburgh received the land in Lauder while the abbey of St James took over the patronage of Bozeat, paying to the canons two and a half merks a year. The king made gifts to the new abbey of the churches of Lanark, Pettinain and Cadisleya, while Lessuden, now St Boswells, was granted to Dryburgh by some person unknown as the confirmation in 1161 by Pope Alexander III bears witness. This possession was the subject of disputes for many years, the earliest of which was settled in 1177 with a promise by the canons of Dryburgh to pay two merks a year to the abbey of Jedburgh.

These are only a few of the many grants made to the abbey during the first century of its existence but are sufficient to illustrate the way it, like other religious houses, gathered property, thus tending to lose the primitive simplicity of the foundation. There is no indication how the canons administered their scattered possessions, a work which must have encroached upon their other labours. For the churches they seem usually to have appointed secular vicars, a part of whose duty, sometimes disputed as will be seen later, was to collect the dues on the church lands out of which only a small sum was allowed them for stipend. Not being an enclosed order they could, however, serve as vicars themselves.

Early abbots
Unlike Melrose, Dryburgh seems never to have possessed any inmates of outstanding sanctity. Separation from the highways by the River Tweed and by the hills behind may account for an uneventful history. Of the early days we find little save the bald entries of the *Chronicle of Melrose*. The writers of this book wasted no time on things too familiar to be interesting; hence we have no idea of the number of original inmates or of the progress of the building.

The day after the canons came into residence in 1152 they appointed their first abbot, Roger. He held office for an unusually

long period, during which the abbey seems to have enjoyed favour at Rome for three bulls were obtained from Pope Alexander III. Of these one bestowed a great privilege— permission to hold divine service in such time as the country lay under interdict, provided that it was celebrated behind closed doors, without ringing of bells and excluding all interdicted and excommunicated persons. Roger continued in office till 1177, when he resigned and his prior, Gerard, was elected in his place.

Abbot Gerard's successor is known mainly from the records of the Carthusian Order of which he became a member. During Gerard's last illness the monastery elected Adam, one of their number, known as 'an exemplary religious' and an excellent preacher, to take his place. He refused to become abbot while Gerard was alive, but apparently held that office for a short time after Gerard's death, between 1184 and 1190. While on a visit to Prémontré and during a preaching tour he fell in love with the Carthusian life at Val St Pierre. Upon his return to England he applied for and received admission to the Charterhouse at Witham, Somerset, where he ended his days. In addition to being a preacher he was also a writer and not a few of his works are known to belong to the days when he was a canon of Dryburgh.

Of subsequent abbots little is recorded. During the tenure of office of Abbot Oliver, mention of whom is made in 1262 and 1268, the daughter-houses in Ireland were . founded.

The *Chronicle of Melrose* describes in detail how Abbot Oliver went to England as an envoy to Prince Edward, later Edward I, from his sister Margaret, queen of Alexander III. The abbot was kept there under close observation by Simon de Montfort, in whose hands the prince was virtually a prisoner.

The abbey's early history
Until the time of the death of Alexander III in 1286, Dryburgh seems to have been little concerned with affairs of state. From the chartulary may be learned that the inmates

View of the abbey ruins from beside the river. In the left foreground is the gate-house; beyond lie the cloisters.

found considerable occupation in matters concerning their lands. Dryburgh was in no way different from other religious houses, accumulating lands and quarrelling over them with an intensity worthy of a better cause. One long dispute concerned the lands in Lauderdale gifted by the De Morevilles.

The patronage of this church was disputed with the abbot by John Balliol, though ultimately he resigned to the canons his right upon condition that they maintained the six chaplains celebrating divine service for the souls of himself and his wife, Devorgilla, and those of their ancestors and descendants.

All available evidence proves the prosperity of the community. Though grants of land are fewer after the first century of its life, the charters of the succeeding period show that the abbey was held in high esteem. It seems also to have been looked upon as a peaceful refuge for those weary of the world and anxious to prepare for the next, as indicated by the charter of Henry de Besingham, who granted certain lands in Thirlestane to supply a pittance to his brethren, the abbot and monastery.

During this period the matter of the possession by abbeys of parish churches was the subject of legislation by the bishop of St Andrews. So far as the matter concerns Dryburgh, we learn that the abbot and monastery were allowed to serve their parishes of Kilrenny, Saltoun, Gullane and Channelkirk with their own canons, should the secular vicars prove troublesome. Otherwise they were obliged to make appointments at a stated stipend.

In national conflicts Dryburgh was also involved. To assist Edward I of England in making his decision between the claimants to the throne of Scotland, commissioners or auditors to the number of 104 were nominated, and among these is noted the prior of Dryburgh.

The abbey in later years

The wars of independence reacted seriously upon the abbey, for in 1322 it was burned by the retreating forces of Edward II after that king's second unsuccessful invasion. It is said that his troops heard the bells of the abbey ringing and that, incensed by the obvious rejoicing, they turned aside to burn the place. A simpler, if more prosaic reason, might be suggested—that the troops had endeavoured to provision themselves there and, failing to do so, had set fire to the abbey out of revenge. The destruction seems to have been considerable for though Robert I is said to have repaired the abbey as he did that of Melrose, and though the parish church of Maxton was granted to the monastery by John, bishop of Glasgow, in 1326 'because it is an act of piety to succour the needy', yet in 1330 Patrick, a canon of the house, recorded the catastrophe in a poem addressed to the king and the superiors of other religious houses—evidently an appeal for funds.

Though a small matter among the grave affairs of the kingdom, it is perhaps worth noting internal trouble in the monastery, as recorded for the first time. A commission from Avignon, dated 1320, records the suspension of Marcus, one of the canons, for knocking down the abbot with his fist. The record is brief; the cause of the episode is not noted nor its termination.

The destruction of the abbey seemed to revive the gifts of the faithful. Besides his other help Robert I had granted to the community a sum of money from the burgh of Roxburgh; Sir Andrew Moray, his friend and brother-in-law, gave up his claim to a piece of land in dispute between him and the abbey, adding thereto free rights of milling and pasturage for 300 sheep. John Maxwell of Pentcaitland added to its possessions the patronage of the church of Pentcaitland.

The Border was not yet free from

A seventeenth-century depiction of a Premonstratensian canon. From the rich vestments and fur stole it will be seen that the original ideas of simplicity in the foundation of the order had been lost. (From W Dugdale, Monasticon Anglicanum, *1655–73).*

disturbance and this fact may account for the incompleteness of the records of Dryburgh. Abbot Andrew with the other three abbots of Teviotdale, was present at Edward Balliol's resignation of the kingdom into the hands of Edward III at Roxburgh on 20 January 1355. By their submission they saved their abbeys while others, such as Haddington, suffered during the English king's march to Edinburgh to demand the allegiance of the Scottish nobles.

The troubles of the period of war were reflected in great laxity of discipline in the abbey, to deal with which the abbot received special powers from Rome.

Dryburgh, as has been shown, produced few persons of great note; yet about this time the convent sheltered one whose fame was not confined to Scotland. About 1354 Ralph Strode, poet and philsopher, lived in the abbey. He was sent by King David II to study

A late medieval vaulting boss which appears to show, with delightful simplicity, the crucification of St Andrew.

A late medieval vaulting boss showing a female head with what appears to be a crimped wimple.

at Merton Collage, Oxford, where he became a fellow. He was known to Chaucer, who inscribed the conclusion of *Troilus and Cresseide* to his friend Gower and 'the philosophical Strode'. Strode visited France, Germany, Italy—where he knew Petrarch—and the Holy Land. He was an opponent of John Wycliffe, a member of the Order of the Preaching Friars and poet laureate at Oxford. But though Strode's work took him far from Scotland it was at Dryburgh that his worth was first recognised.

Edward III's kindness to Dryburgh outlasted the return of David II from captivity, for in 1373 the canons had a warrant from him to ship 80 sacks of Scots wool at Berwick for payment of half a merk a sack. This may not have been a mere favour; the capture of Berwick by the English had meant the loss of its importance as Scotland's chief port while the great traffic in Border wool had been diverted, largely by the foresight of Robert the Bruce, to Edinburgh's port of Leith. But Abbot Andrew lived to see the perilous favour of England lost when, in retaliation for the invasion of England by the Scots and French under Sir John de Vienne, Richard II raided Scotland in 1385. As ever, the Border abbeys suffered and Dryburgh among them is reported to have been 'devastated by hostile fire'. The damage was extensive, probably almost disastrous, and it seems that the abbey never regained its lost

splendour. Yet Robert III, following the example of his predecessor, first of the name, endeavoured to compensate the canons by a grant of the lands and revenues of the Cistercian priory of Berwick-on-Tweed, whose nuns were accused of dissolute living and their convent broken up.

During the fifteenth century the abbey again was much occupied with disputes. There were lawsuits with adjoining landowners, too trivial to note in detail, yet significant as showing the trend of the age, a growing disrespect for the monastic orders, if not for the church. That such disrespect was far from being unfounded even Dryburgh's history shows.

Andrew Lidderdale, it seems, was the last abbot and, after his death in 1507, the abbey was held merely *in commendam*. James Stewart, natural son of Master John Stewart and rector of Ancrum, was legitimised to qualify him for the office but the election does not seem to have been completed. In 1509 the canons petitioned James IV to prefer David Finlayson, a canon of the house and vicar of Gullane, one of their own churches. Their request was ignored, the abbey remained vacant and the first of the commendators was appointed.

The commendators and the Reformation

Nominations *in commendam*, originally appointments of a person to levy the fruits of a benefice during a vacancy, became during the reigns of James IV and James V a habitual practice and a scandal. Abbeys and other benefices were granted to laymen, frequently the illegitimate sons of the king, for the purpose of securing them an establishment, or obtained and held by influential churchmen.

The first commendator of Dryburgh was the great ecclesiastic and diplomat, Andrew Forman. Pope Julius II provided him to Dryburgh in 1509 on the king's nomination, and he held it, with other benefices, for some years.

David Hamilton, bishop of Argyll, natural son of James, Lord Hamilton, and half brother of James, earl of Arran, became commendator in 1518. The bishopric of Argyll was not a rich one; probably the revenue of Dryburgh, then estimated at 400 florins, was a welcome addition to his income. Hamilton died in 1522, not long before war again ravaged the Borders. The raids of the earl of Surrey laid waste Merse and Teviotdale; Lord Dacre plundered the neighbourhood of Kelso; Jedburgh was burned shortly afterwards. How far Dryburgh suffered is not definitely stated though an unsigned letter of 1523, attributable to the Regent Albany and directed to the Cardinal Protector of Scotland at the papal court, urged the appointment of a superior who could give his whole attention to the affairs and repair of the abbey.

The manner in which the appointment was carried out is an interesting comment on ecclesiastical patronage of the period. Dryburgh was bestowed by the regent on John Stewart, second son of the earl of Lennox. He was a minor, and the earl and he bestowed the commendatorship on James Stewart, canon of Glasgow, with the provisions that he should become an Augustinian canon—a condition seemingly ignored—and that he should pay to the earl's son a pension of £500 Scots. How far so large a pension could be made consistent with the reason for his appointment, the repair of the abbey, does not appear. Yet he seems to have

The coat-of-arms of James Stewart, son of the earl of Lennox, over the south-west door into the cloisters. The first and fourth quarters contain the Stewart fess checky, the second and the third the arms of France. In the centre is the Lennox shield: a red cross with four flowers.

done some building for his coat-of-arms can still be seen above the south-west door of the cloister.

Stewart died in 1541 and was succeeded by Thomas Erskine, second son of John, Lord Erskine, to whose family the abbey thereafter belonged.

The Erskines

The case of Dryburgh illustrates the tendency for church lands to become hereditary in the possession of nobles or landed gentry, though the sons of Lord Erskine were more fortunate than others in their uninterrupted possession of the abbey lands. For when Robert, master of Erskine, was killed at Pinkie in 1547 and Thomas, the commendator, became heir to their father, the younger brother, John, succeeded without question to Dryburgh.

Before that, however, Dryburgh suffered again from the attacks of the 'ancient enemy'. The earl of Hertford's invasion of Scotland in 1544 did much damage on the Border. A letter from Thomas Erskine reported that the earl of Angus had convened most of the gentry of Lothian to pass to the Border for resisting the English, and stated that he himself was on his way to Dryburgh, presumably to assemble his tenantry for the same purpose. A further letter to the queen dowager (Mary of Guise), dated 12 September 1544, reported the great damage done by the English and 'speciallie besyde my place quhar thai have destroyit all the teindis that I had in thai partis . . .' Because of this he and the monastery had nothing left to sustain them but their property in Lothian, of which Lord Bothwell had taken possession without consent either of the writer or the monastery—a distressing precedent followed by others in the neighbourhood.

This misfortune was followed by a greater one which a contemporary English writer describes. On Friday, 4 November 1544, Sir George Bowes, Sir Brian Layton and others to the number of 700 men 'rode into Scotland upon the water of Tweide to a town called Dryburgh with an abbey in the same, which was a pretty town and well buylded; and they burnte the same town and abbey, saving the churche, with a great substance of corne and gote very much spoylage and insicht geir and brought away an hundredth nolte, sixty nagges, a hundreth sheip . . . and they tarried so long as the said burnynge and spoylage that it was Satterday at eight of the cloke at nycht or they come home'. The abbey and town were never rebuilt.

In the same year the commendator took revenge in a raid across the Border where some damage was done before the Scottish forces retreated. Possibly it was in retaliation for this raid that Erskine, captured in March, 1547, at sea on his way to France, was detained a prisoner in England despite the protests of the queen dowager and the Regent Arran. During his captivity the battle of Pinkie was fought and by the death of his elder brother, Thomas became master of Erskine and heir to his father, Lord Erskine. He resigned his commendatorship in favour of his brother, John, but predeceased his father and the new commendator succeeded his father in 1554 as the sixth Lord Erskine.

His subsequent history and promotion to the earldom of Mar do not concern the abbey.

In 1556 his place was filled by another member of the house of Erskine, David, natural son of Robert, master of Erskine, and thus nephew of both preceding commendators. He was also commendator of Inchmahome Priory in Perthshire. In his time the Reformation took place. It seems to have come to the abbey without any perceptible clash, possibly because David sided with the reformers, following the example of his uncle, the earl of Mar. David is described as 'an exceedingly modest, honest and shame-faced man'. Like his immediate predecessors his life was led far from the abbey. To a considerable extent he was involved in the politics of that vexed period; he accompanied the Lords of the Congregation in Leith in 1571 when the queen's adherents held the capital on her behalf. He was present at the Parliament of the King's Lords in the Canongate in 1572, though he helped to defend Jedburgh from Ferniehirst and Buccleuch in the same year. By the act of that parliament electing John, earl of Mar, tutor to the young King James VI, the commendator of Dryburgh was named one of his assistants. Probably because of that appointment he lived chiefly in Stirling Castle, the home of the king. He was a member of the Privy Council in 1579 but in 1582 was implicated in the Raid of Ruthven and forced to flee to England. His estates were confiscated but four years later he was reinstated.

During all these years there is little to record of the abbey itself. Though it can never have regained its past prosperity there is evidence from its rent-roll that it was a property worth retaining. In 1561 the revenue in money was £912 3s. 4d. Scots, besides large payments in kind. In 1567 the third payable from the abbey lands for the support of the ministers of the reformed church was £304, apart from dues in kind.

The number of canons in residence dwindled. From 1537 onwards, when at least 17 canons and their abbot are recorded, leases and other documents were signed by

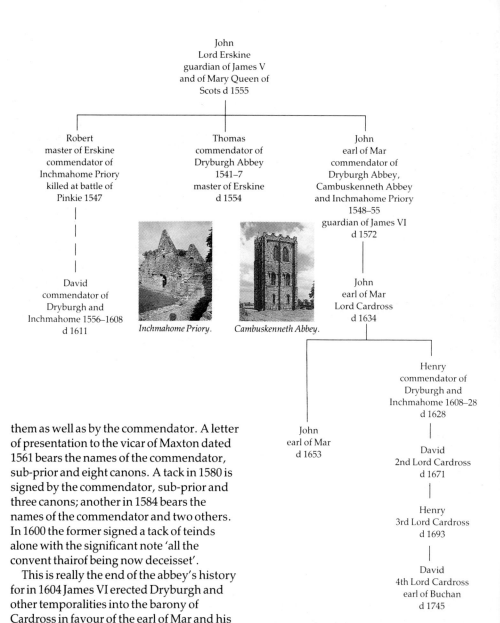

John
Lord Erskine
guardian of James V
and of Mary Queen of
Scots d 1555

Robert
master of Erskine
commendator of
Inchmahome Priory
killed at battle of
Pinkie 1547

Thomas
commendator of
Dryburgh Abbey
1541–7
master of Erskine
d 1554

John
earl of Mar
commendator of
Dryburgh Abbey,
Cambuskenneth Abbey
and Inchmahome Priory
1548–55
guardian of James VI
d 1572

David
commendator of
Dryburgh and
Inchmahome 1556–1608
d 1611

Inchmahome Priory.

Cambuskenneth Abbey.

John
earl of Mar
Lord Cardross
d 1634

John
earl of Mar
d 1653

Henry
commendator of
Dryburgh and
Inchmahome 1608–28
d 1628

David
2nd Lord Cardross
d 1671

Henry
3rd Lord Cardross
d 1693

David
4th Lord Cardross
earl of Buchan
d 1745

them as well as by the commendator. A letter of presentation to the vicar of Maxton dated 1561 bears the names of the commendator, sub-prior and eight canons. A tack in 1580 is signed by the commendator, sub-prior and three canons; another in 1584 bears the names of the commendator and two others. In 1600 the former signed a tack of teinds alone with the significant note 'all the convent thairof being now deceisset'.

This is really the end of the abbey's history for in 1604 James VI erected Dryburgh and other temporalities into the barony of Cardross in favour of the earl of Mar and his sons. To the commendator was reserved the life rent which he had enjoyed by royal grant since the annexation of the church lands to the crown in 1587.

David Erskine died in 1611, leaving a widow and children to the protection of the earl of Mar, and to his nominal office succeeded Henry, second son of the earl.

With his death the ecclesiastical title disappeared and the abbey fell to his son David, Lord Cardross. He sold part of the lands to Dryburgh's old rivals, the Haliburtons of Newmains and is said to have resided in the abbey buildings till his death in 1671.

A drawing by Captain James Alexander of the funeral procession of Sir Walter Scott passing Dryburgh Abbey on 26 September 1832.

His successor, the third Lord Cardross, favouring the Covenant party, held conventicles in his house of Dryburgh, over at least one of which presided Henry Erskine, father of Ralph and Ebenezer, leaders of the Secession Church at a later date. Imprisoned and fined, Lord Cardross sold Dryburgh to Sir Patrick Scott of Ancrum and emigrated to South Carolina.

In 1700 the abbey passed to the hands of Thomas Haliburton of Newmains; Robert Haliburton, grand-uncle of Sir Walter Scott, becoming bankrupt, sold it to Lieutenant-Colonel Charles Tod, whose daughters sold it in 1786 to the earl of Buchan, a descendant of Henry, Lord Cardross. From his heirs it was acquired for the nation by the gift of Lord Glenconner in 1919.

Tombstone in the north transept of one of Sir Walter Scott's ancestors, John Haliburton, who died in 1640.

31

Ashlar stone walling of the highest quality, with blocks of regular size, perfectly squared, well faced and finely pointed.

Aumbry a recess or cupboard in a wall.

Barrel-vault continuous vault resembling a tunnel.

Clerestory a range of windows in the highest part of the church.

Cloister a covered way or arcade enclosing a quadrangle.

Commendator a secular head of an ecclesiastical property.

Corbel projecting stone to support a timber beam or overhanging wall.

Cusps the projecting points made by the arcs of Gothic tracery.

Engaged shaft a shaft or column attached to a wall.

Lancet a narrow window opening with a pointed arch head.

Piscina a perforated stone basin for carrying away water used in rinsing altar vessels.

Skew-putt a corbel stone at the bottom of a skew, the coping to a gable wall.

Spandrel a triangular surface area between the apexes of two arches.

Springer the bottom, or beginning, of the curve of an arch or vault.

Subcroft an undercroft or basement of a building.

Tracery the decorative masonry within the head of a Gothic window, forming leaf-life shapes.

Transepts the north and south arms of a cruciform church, normally the same height as the nave.

Water-table a horizontal offset in a wall, sloped on the upper surface to throw off water.

Further Reading

Royal Commission on Ancient and Historical Monuments of Scotland *Inventory of Berwickshire* (Edinburgh 1915).

Ian B Cowan and David E Easson *Medieval Religious Houses: Scotland* (London 1976).

Stewart Cruden *Scottish Medieval Churches* (Edinburgh 1986).

R Fawcett, *Scottish Medieval Churches* (Edinburgh 1985).

© Crown copyright 1983

First published 1937
Fourth edition 1987
Second impression 1991

ISBN 0 11 493407 X

Printed in Scotland for HMSO
Dd.287724   HF4719   3M   6/91   37907

CLASSIC COMPETITION MOTORCYCLES

CLASSIC COMPETITION MOTORCYCLES

From The National Motorcycle Museum

Bob Currie

Patrick Stephens
Wellingborough, Northamptonshire

First published in 1987

British Library Cataloguing in Publication Data

Currie, Bob
   Classic motorcyles of the National Motorcycle
   Museum.
   1. Motorcycles — History
   I. Title
   629.2′275′0904   TL440

   ISBN 0-85059-880-X

*Patrick Stephens Limited is part of the
Thorsons Publishing Group*

Printed and bound in Italy

Contents

Introduction — the world of competition

Competitive motorcycling, the desperate need to demonstrate that 'my bike's better than your bike', has been with us ever since the very dawn of powered two-wheeling. True, man has an inborn competitive spirit — the caveman who clobbered the juiciest brontosaurus was the hero of his tribe — but it was a little more than that. Early motorcycle builders were working in a hitherto unexplored field, exposure to competition brought to light weaknesses in their products that may not have shown up in normal use, and as these were eradicated so a better machine resulted.

Naturally enough, early race meetings took place on board-surfaced cycledromes because, like Mount Everest, they were there. In Paris there was the Parc aux Princes track; nearer to home cycle race venues such as Herne Hill, Crystal Palace, Aston Villa and New Brighton Tower were employed and it was there that the Collier brothers (Harry and Charlie) with their Plumstead-built Matchlesses, Sam Wright and Harry Martin with MMC-powered Excelsiors, and C. F. Crundall and his P&M-type Humber first came to prominence.

Cycledromes had their limitations, for though they were fine so long as speeds remained relatively low, as motorcycle power outputs increased so the inadequacies of the short tracks became more and more evident and by the mid-1900s that particular form of sport had already had its day.

But in any case, motorcycle racing was moving on. International (or to be more accurate, inter-nation) sport began in 1904 with the Coupe Internationale in which three-man teams were selected to represent the competing countries, but the ruthless continentals indulged in so much skulduggery — nails strewn in the paths of opposing riders, mechanics with supplies of spares hiding themselves in strategic locations, and goodness knows that else — that the 'Coupe' series came to an ignominious close after only three years. In any case, it was felt that with massive engines housed in the most rudimentary of frames, the event was leading motorcycle design into a cul-de-sac. Yet what could take its place?

Ah, now! This is where the Marquis de Mazoully de St Mars (Britain's official observer at the Coupe Internationale meetings) had a brainwave. He would present a magnificent trophy for a different kind of race — one which, he foresaw, would help the development of the ordinary touring motorcycle; for that reason he called his award the Tourist Trophy. It would take place over a circuit of everyday roads, with corners and hills, so that handling, braking, acceleration and so on would be given a true test.

Because of the negative attitude of the British Government to motor sport (indeed to the motor vehicle as such) there was nowhere on the mainland where such an event could be staged. But the Isle of Man had its own parliament, and was quite willing to pass an Act whereby the main roads of the Island could be barred to normal traffic in order that a race could take place without hindrance.

So, in 1907, the TT Races came into being. Initially these were over ten laps of a 13-mile circuit in the west of the Island, because although competitors had to struggle up the sharp rise of Creg Willey's Hill (today better known to TT enthusiasts as Sarah's Cottage) the course was less gruelling than the longer Mountain course which had already been employed for car trials. Nevertheless, the first TT events were not straightforward races as we know them today. Bear in mind that the TT was intended to develop the touring machine, so although speed came into it competitors were given only a limited fuel allowance; it was a matter of whether to go flat-out all the way and risk running out of fuel, or play safe with the throttle and settle for a reasonably respectable finish. Moreover, before the race each machine had to pass a 'standard of silence test', being ridden at set speed past a table at which were seated an ACU panel who, unaided by noise meters or similar scientific gadgetry, passed judgement by ear alone.

Of course the restrictions didn't last long and, especially after the move to the $37\frac{3}{4}$-mile Mountain Course (with its climb from Ramsey to the often mist-shrouded slopes of Snaefell) the TT Races did indeed play a significant part in motorcycle development, perfecting the countershaft gearbox, the overhead-valve (and, later, overhead-camshaft) engine, forks, brakes, tyres, transmissions and exhaust systems.

However, the TT was not the only catalyst, for in 1906 a far-sighted Surrey estate owner, Mr Hugh Locke-King, laid out on his land at Weybridge a huge concrete speed track with banked turns. This was Brooklands, the world's first purpose-built motor sport venue, though it has to be said that it was appreciated more by competitors than by spectators. The scale of Brooklands was too vast for a race (especially, a motorcycle race) to offer any sort of spectacle — 'like flippin' flies crawling round a flippin' saucer' was one description. But it offered a venue for speed-record attempts; not for out-and-out World Land Speed Record attempts, for which the firm sands of Pendine Beach in South Wales were more suited, but for capacity-class time or distance records such as the 350 cc One-hour, or 500 cc Sidecar 100-mile.

In fact quite a little coterie of specialist record-attempters based themselves at Brooklands, each taking care to break the existing record by as small a margin as practicable so that Fred, or Bill, could have a fair crack at it next time round. It was lucrative, in that the advertising value of a broken record brought monetary reward (the riders called it 'Bonii') from the makers of the tyres, oils, spark plugs and any other relevant items used in the ride.

But whether Brooklands played much of a part in the development of the motorcycle is doubtful. The traffic was all one-way, so steering and braking were of little importance; and as for gearboxes, well, once a bike had been taken up through the gears to its racing speed, that was it until the chequered flag went out.

Let's backtrack half a dozen paragraphs or so. The Isle of Man was the home of the TT Races, because it was illegal to close the public roads of the British mainland for competitive sport. True enough, but nonetheless speed trials (we would call them sprints today) and hill climbs were held on the open roads until the mid-1920s, with the authorities turning a blind eye to such goings-on and, indeed, with the local police often helping to keep the highway clear for runs to be made.

Kop Hill near Princes Risborough; Spion Kop near Rugeley; Sutton Bank near Thirsk; Angel Bank, Ludlow; Chatcombe Pitch near Cheltenham — these and many more acclivities became the Meccas of the speed hill climb specialists like Freddie Dixon and George Dance. It was possible because everyday traffic then was so light as to be almost non-existent. Until World War 1, anyway, country dwellers rarely travelled further than the next village (and even then the journey would be on foot or horseback) and the average traffic flow would perhaps be one car and two carts per hour, if that. So an event on the public road inconvenienced few, any traffic being held until there was a convenient break in the programme before being allowed to proceed.

After World War 1 it was rather different. As traffic flows began to rise so it became more and more obvious that main-road sport would have to end — a decision hastened in 1925 by a nasty accident at Kop Hill. Some sprints and hill climbs did carry on, but transferred to the drives of stately homes including Madresfield Court, Malvern and Luton Hoo. A few of these events, such as Hoghton Towers, survive to this day.

Trials — give them their full and illuminating original name of reliability trials and we gain an insight into their purpose — are the oldest branch of motorcycle competition of all, for they can be dated right back to the Automobile Club's great 1,000-mile Reliability Trial of 1900 (a car event, but the entries did include a couple of motor tricycles and a quadricycle). That particular event was more of a mobile Motor Show than anything else but at least it was a start, and before very long true reliability trials had come into being.

In essence these were out-and-back affairs on ordinary roads, which a competitor had to complete without an involuntary stop — not too easy in those days when valves would stretch and have to be replaced at the roadside, and accumulators would shake to pieces with the vibration of it all. As better metals came into use and machines grew gradually more efficient, so trials organizers became more adventurous, including a hill or two in the route. (Dashwood, for example, the rise out of West Wycombe towards Oxford, was favourite in early ACU Quarterly Trials, the route of which ran from Uxbridge to Banbury Cross and back.)

Six-Days Trials were another variation, in which competitors travelled around the country with a different stopping place each night. The ACU Six-Days, Scottish Six-Days, and even the early International Six-Days Trials all followed this format, the machines employed being the standard road models of the time.

Motorcycles were improving all the while, and in consequence trials organizers had to devise stiffer and yet stiffer tests to demonstrate the capabilities of the machines and (increasingly) the skills of their riders. Success in the major trials was trumpeted in press advertising and in posters displayed in motorcycle shops throughout the country, and sales of the victorious makes increased proportionally.

But in the course of time all motorcycles came to be reliable. Organizers ran out of suitably steep and tortuous public roads against which the machines could be pitted and were forced to look instead for hazards situated on private land — stream beds, rock-filled gulleys, steep and muddy farm tracks, and tricky twists and turns among the saplings. In a sense it could be likened to mechanized show-jumping, the laurels going to those who cleared the most hazards, but by now it was the rider who was the star, not the machine he chanced to be riding and the sales value of a trials win (in so far as road machines were concerned) was virtually nil.

The second great off-road form of motorcycle sport, once known as scrambling but now more commonly called moto-cross, started as an offshoot of trials. Whereas in trials the emphasis is on the slow-motion skill of the rider in tackling an observed section without dropping a foot, in moto-cross speed is of the essence. The modern name is derived from 'motorcycle cross-country', and if trials can be likened to show-jumping, then moto-cross is steeplechasing (indeed some of the longer-established events still retain a Grand National·label).

The sport has come a long way in a comparatively short space of time, and each branch has developed its own specialized type of machine. In the pages which follow you will meet the most representative gathering of competition machines to be found anywhere in the world, each and every one displayed at the National Motorcycle Museum, and here beautifully pictured by the lens of Jim Davies.

1938 346 cc AJS 7R

Call it luck, or call it a happy accident, but when Colliers, the Plumstead-based manufacturer of Matchless motorcycles, acquired the AJS marque in 1931 they had no intention of continuing the overhead-camshaft 346 cc Model 7 (and the corresponding 500 cc Model 10). However, AJS works rider George Rowley, who had moved south from Wolverhampton at the takeover, got wind of one of the old A. J. Stevens company's works racers that had been shipped back from Italy and was being held at Dover pending payment of freight charges. George slipped down at Dover, paid the outstanding debt himself and brought the bike back to the factory where he hid it from the bosses' eye.

The model was in good order so, without telling his employers, he entered it for the Brooklands 100-mile Grand Prix. Publication of the entry list, showing works rider Rowley on an AJS, alerted the weekly motorcycle press, which speculated in print as to whether this meant re-entry of AJS officially into the racing field. In the race, George finished fifth in the 350 cc class, and would have done better still had it not been for a bunged-up fuel line. That had the unexpected result that the company chairman sent for George, congratulated him on his performance, and told him that Colliers had had second thoughts. They would, after all, bring back the overhead-camshaft models and, furthermore, would continue development.

Ancestry of the engine dated from 1926, when the A. J. Stevens concern's then-young chief engineer, Phil Walker, had laid out an engine in which the single overhead camshaft was driven by a long chain tensioned by a Weller spring-loaded blade (a system first used on a racing Aston Martin car engine). Walker, like Rowley, had joined the Plumstead staff, and now he was given the task of taking his original design further.

The significant year was 1936, when the revamped Model 7 was shown on the AJS stand at the Olympia Show, with the promise of production after the 1937 TT period. Originally located ahead of the crankcase, the magneto was now transferred to a platform at the rear of the cylinder and, in consequence, the timing chaincase had taken on a configuration that would be echoed in the post-war Model 7R. Other changes included hairpin valve springs, a downdraught carburettor and a four-speed footchange Burman gearbox. The 500 cc version was dropped.

True to their word, the company announced in late June 1937 that the 346 cc Model 7 Racing (or in catalogue terms, the 37/7R) was entering small-quantity production — 'expressly for riders with a fair amount of racing experience, and who are capable of maintaining a rather super kind of power unit'. Essentially it was a replica of works TT model and came complete with a 4½-gallon tank, racing footrests and straight-through exhaust with large megaphone. Each model was to be personally tested at Brooklands by George Rowley before dispatch, and the price would be £87 5s.

The 1938 works racers moved even nearer to post-war specification by adopting a duplex cradle frame and plunger rear springing, but this benefit was not passed through to the production 7R, which continued with the older type of single tube diamond frame. It was, said the firm, exactly similar to the machine which had gained second, third and the team prize in the Ulster Grand Prix; but the price had risen to £94 10s.

Specification

Make AJS. **Model** 38/7R. **Engine** 346 cc (70 × 90 mm bore and stroke) single overhead-camshaft single. **Power output** Not quoted. **Tyres** 3.00 × 21 in front and rear. **Frame** Brazed-lug tubular diamond. **Suspension** Girder front fork with friction dampers. Rigid rear. **Weight** Not quoted. **Wheelbase** 54 in. **Manufacturer** Associated Motor Cycles Ltd, Plumstead Road, London SE18.

Above The AJS factory had built chain-driven ohc models since 1926, but 1938 was the first year the 7R designation was employed. **Right** 'Built expressly for riders with a fair amount of racing experience', claimed the AJS catalogue — and the 1938 Model 7R certainly looked the part. **Far right** The chain-driven overhead camshaft, with Weller chain tensioner, was continued into post-World War 2 Model 7R production. **Below** Essentially a replica of the factory's own works racers, each 7R was personally tested at Brooklands by George Rowley.

1948 348 cc AJS 7R

One couldn't really claim the post-war 7R AJS to have been a world-beater; but in truth it was never intended to be. It was, pure and simple, a bike for the lads — the weekend racers who made up the bulk of every meeting. Straightforward in construction, it was easy to work on, even in a muddy paddock with no more shelter than a tarpaulin. And possessed of a useful amount of power, it gave its rider a more than reasonable chance of getting in among the prize money. The customers at whom it was aimed appreciated the model, and within weeks of its announcement it had been given the unofficial name it was to carry for its life span — the Boys' Racer.

The 'Model 7 Racing' had been in production pre-war, of course, and its reintroduction for the 1948 season was greeted with tremendous enthusiasm. But though the model was obviously derived from the pre-war bike, and retained the familiar Weller-tensioned chain drive to a single overhead camshaft, it was in most other respects a wholly new design. Once again it was the work of AMC's chief engineer Phil Walker, whose association with the 'cammy Ajay' went all the way back to 1926. It would remain in production — changed and improved from time to time — right through to 1962, though in later years development would be in the hands of first Ike Hatch and, finally, Jack Williams.

Bore and stroke dimensions of the 1948 Model 7R were 74×81 mm (the same as those of the Mk VIII KTT Velocette, incidentally), giving 348 cc capacity, and the iron-lined cylinder barrel was spigoted very deeply into the high mouth of the magnesium-alloy crankcase castings. The same magnesium-alloy was employed for the camshaft-drive casing and cambox, and because mag-alloy is subject to corrosion when exposed to salt air (such as, for instance, when treated as deck cargo on the Isle of Man steamer!) it was given a special protective coating of gold-coloured inhibiting paint. That the gilding resulted in a most distinctive and remarkably handsome finish was sheer coincidence.

Running in a pair of ball journal bearings, the single camshaft, was accommodated in a light but massive cambox casting, and at its driven end there was a vernier arrangement (similar to that used on AJS magneto drives since the early 1920s) to give fine tuning adjustment. Rocker arms were carried on eccentric pins, to provide a simple method of setting the valve clearances.

Coupled to a four-speed gearbox with a short gearchange pedal, the engine was housed in an all-welded duplex loop frame with, at the rear, angled hydraulic damper units of AMC's own manufacture. Adding to the appearance of the machine was a megaphone of possibly the largest diameter of all time.

Appearance of the 7R was eagerly awaited, and it was sales manager (and pre-war racing star) Jock West who gave the model its first public showing, by completing several laps of Brands Hatch — at that time still a grass track venue. But the factory had promised ample supplies in good time for the 1948 TT and, sure enough, as riders in the Junior event took station on the grid, the distinguished black and gold livery was strongly in evidence. Four eager beavers even entered their 'three-fifties' for the Senior TT — and Geoff Murdoch actually brought his into a resounding fourth place. The 7R was, very definitely, on its way!

Specification

Make AJS. **Model** 48/7R. **Engine** 348 cc (74×81 mm bore and stroke) single overhead-camshaft single. **Power output** 31 bhp at 7,000 rpm. **Tyres** 3.00×21 in front, 3.25×20 in rear. **Frame** All-welded twin tubular cradle, with single top tube. **Suspension** Oil-damped telescopic front forks. Swinging arm rear forks controlled by spring and hydraulic units. **Weight** 298 lb dry. **Wheelbase** 55.5 in. **Manufacturer** Associated Motor Cycles Ltd, Plumstead Road, London SE18.

Above Soon to be dubbed the 'Boy's Racer' — because it gave the average club racing man a chance to be in the money — the AJS Model 7R grew to be the best-loved comp model of all time.
Right Shrouded Teledraulic front forks, and a small wire-mesh flyscreen were expected on a 1948 road racer; fairings came much later. **Far right** Like its pre-war counterpart, the 7R employed chain drive to the overhead camshaft. The gold finish was protective rather than decorative.
Below Over the years (it stayed in production until 1962), the 348 cc AJS was to change in many subtle ways.

1958 347 cc AJS 16MC Trials

Present-day trials are so dominated by agile lightweight machines, that those who were not followers of the sport af the time might well gape in astonishment when told that right through the 1950s and into the early 1960s, the models which ruled the trials roost were ungainly-looking singles such as the AJS Model 16MC.

It was indeed so, though, and it was on a long-stroke 347 cc AJS — a rigid-frame model at that — that Hugh Viney won the Scottish Six-Days Trial three times on the trot (1947, 1948, and 1949) then added one more win for luck in 1953. In 1955 rear springing — a swinging arm system, controlled by the famous 'jampot' damper units of AMC's own design and make — was added to the AJS trials model; and if that sounds a little late in the day, the reason was that trials riders of the time believed that a rigid frame allowed the engine to deliver its punch to the rear wheel more directly, and so gave them more grip. Poppycock, of course, as they were soon to discover.

It was a Kentish farmer, Gordon Jackson, who now took on the discarded mantle of Viney and he, too, was to win the 'Scottish' four times (in 1956, 1958, 1960 and 1961). That final win was his most celebrated outing of all, for he completed the entire six days at the cost of just one solitary lost mark.

By 1957 the Model 16MC had acquired a new and lighter all-welded frame, and the AMC rear dampers had been replaced by proprietary Girling components. The new frame offered a very acceptable ground clearance of 10 in, and further protection from possible damage in jagged rockery was provided by a sump bashplate. Seating accommodation was by way of a rather rudimentary Dunlop rubber saddle, but since trials men rarely sat down anyway (except when travelling between observed sections), riding comfort occupied a very low position of importance.

The companion scrambles model had moved to a new short-stroke (72 × 85.5 mm) engine, but the trials machine adhered to the older long-stroke (69 × 93 mm) which, in conjunction with 'soft' cam profiles and a compression ratio of only 6.5 to 1, endowed the model with the 'plonkability' necessary for tackling at slow speed a long and rock-filled gulley.

Ignition was by a Lucas wading magneto, a specially-waterproofed instrument which permitted the machine to ford deepish streams, and no lighting equipment was provided unless ordered specifically (though one model, at least, was so equipped for use in Mountain Rescue). A small fuel tank and light-alloy mudguards helped in all-up weight saving.

Shown here is a 1958 version of the Model 16MC, but there was no significant specification change from 1957. A year later, however, the 16MC adopted a shorter wheelbase and lighter frame based on that used by Gordon Jackson (the saving aided by smaller, single-sided brake drums, instead of the former full-width hubs, was a useful 25 lb) but thereafter there was no major development. Production ended in August 1963.

What the public were unaware of was that Jackson had in fact been using one of the short-stroke (but low compression) scrambles engines in his works mount. But it was decided not to build a genunine Jackson Replica, for not everyone had his throttle-hand skill. Even his team-mates reverted, for preference, to the old long-stroke.

Specification

Make AJS. **Model** 58/16MC Trials. **Engine** 347 cc (69 × 93 mm bore and stroke) overhead-valve single. **Power output** 18 bhp at 5,750 rpm. **Tyres** 2.75 × 21 in front, 4.00 × 19 in rear. **Frame** All-welded tubular crade. **Suspension** Oil-damped telescopic front forks. Swinging-arm rear forks controlled by spring and hydraulic units. **Weight** 319 lb dry. **Wheelbase** 54 in. **Manufacturer** Associated Motor Cycles Ltd, Plumstead Road, London SE18.

Above An impressive string of Scottish Six-Days Trial victories by Hugh Viney and, later, Gordon Jackson, kept the AJS name well to the forefront in the trials world. **Right** Ground clearance was a generous 10 in. **Far right** The all-alloy longstroke motor survived almost to the end of Plumstead production, giving way to a shortstroke engine for the last few seasons. **Below** Not until 1957 did the obstinate AMC management abandon home-built rear dampers in favour of proprietary Girling units — and even then, non-standard lower mountings were necessary.

1957 497 cc Ariel HT5 Trials

No motorcycle in the entire history of trials competition ever amassed such an astounding total of awards, or gathered unto itself such an enthusiastic following, as a certain 497 cc ohv Ariel wearing registration number GOV132 and piloted by one Samuel Hamilton Miller. What is more, Sammy Miller was to go on developing GOV132, and winning yet more trials on it, long after Ariel themselves had ceased to manufacture four-strokes.

True, GOV132 at the close of its reign was a totally different animal to what it had been originally. Stuffed with titanium bits and bobs, clothed in skimpy glass fibre, and featuring the bare minimum of a frame — all aimed at taking the all-up weight of a full-blown 'five-hundred' down below 250 lb — it could never have been produced commercially. Nevertheless, a case could have been made out for producing a near-enough Sammy Miller Replica (and, indeed, charging the earth for it) and the mystery is why the Ariel management didn't show such initiative.

In the beginning, there had been just the one general-purpose Ariel competitions 497 cc model, the VCH, and this served well enough when the sport was less specialized than it became later, but for 1954 the VCH was replaced by two machines, each aimed at its particular branch of motorcycle sport. These were the HS scrambler and the HT trials mount, and whereas the scrambles model featured a duplex cradle frame and a swinging-arm rear suspension system with the fork arms (as on the Ariel roadster models) of rectangular section and fabricated from pressings, the trials bike had a short-wheelbase rigid frame with a single front-down tube.

Both versions employed an all-light-alloy engine derived from that of the road-going Model VHA but, again, there were essential differences (a high-compression piston and road ratios for the Model HS; a low-compression piston and wide-ratio gearbox for the trialer).

Use of a rigid frame for the trials model was dictated by the belief still widely held by riders of the day that rear-springing would somehow interrupt the flow of power from engine to rear tyre. However, Johnny Brittain and his rear-sprung Royal Enfield were proving that this was a fallacy and, gradually, the trials men came to accept that a springer was not such a useless beast after all. The 1956 Model HT, therefore, blossomed forth with a new all-welded lightweight frame which incorporated swinging-arm rear suspension yet at the same time contrived an acceptably short wheelbase. This, then, was where Sammy Miller entered the picture, for it was in the 1956 Scottish Six-Days Trial that he (having originally entered a James) took over the saddle of GOV132. The rest, as they say, is history.

Here we are looking at the 1957 production trials model, by this time known as the HT5 because a corresponding 350 cc version, the HT3, had entered the range. It was much as for the previous season, and was to continue through to the end of its life in 1959 almost without change.

So far, though, we have considered the role of the HT in solo trials, but Miller's mount apart, it was as a sidecar trials model that the 497 cc Ariel finally came into its own. In the hands of Frank Wilkins, Peter Wraith, Alan Morewood or Ron Langston, it so dominated the sidecar trials championships that if you hadn't an Ariel, you weren't taking the game seriously.

Specification

Make Ariel. **Model** HT5 Trials. **Engine** 497 cc (81.8 × 95 mm bore and stroke) overhead-valve single. **Power output** 25 bhp at 6,000 rpm. **Tyres** 2.75 × 21 in front, 4.00 × 19 in rear. **Frame** All-welded tubular diamond. **Suspension** Oil-damped telescopic front forks. Swinging-arm rear forks controlled by spring and hydraulic units. **Weight** 290 lb dry. **Wheelbase** 53 in. **Manufacturer** Ariel Motors Ltd, Grange Road, Selly Oak, Birmingham 29.

Above Heavy (by modern standards) plonking four-stroke singles ruled the trials scene of the 1950s and 1960s, and the handsome Ariel was among the best of 'em. **Right** Seen here in solo form, the 497 cc Ariel really came into its own as a trials sidecar haulier. **Far right** A beautiful example of clean design, the all-light-alloy engine of the Ariel HT5; the gearbox is of Burman make. **Below** The rear-sprung Ariel trials 'five-hundred' was produced from 1956 to 1959 only. Best known of the breed was Sammy Miller's immortal GOV132.

1925 980 cc Brough-Superior SS100 Sprint

Always the showman, George Brough used to advertise his big vee-twins as 'The Rolls-Royce of Motor Cycles' which, in their day, they really were. (It is a fitting footnote to the Brough story that when World War 2 broke out, the Brough-Superior works retooled for the manufacture of precision parts... for Rolls Royce!) But for all the ballyhoo, Brough never made more than perhaps 3,000 machines in all the time he was in business.

Fortunately, the factory records survive, so it can be said with certainty that the 1925 Model SS100 sprinter now in the National Motorcycle Museum collection left the factory at Nottingham on 20 February that year, built to the order of one Charles Needham, of Manchester, a man who was no slouch where sand racing was concerned.

Perhaps the most intriguing episode in the history of this particular Brough-Superior happened in September 1925, in the open championship sand-race meeting staged on Southport Sands in the Mersey estuary, by the Southport MC. 'Most of the super speedmen of the north were present', ran a contemporary report, 'and the speeds were consistently high'. Indeed, the stars of the meeting proved to be Charles Needham and Barry Baragwanath, both on Brough-Superiors, and George Grinton on a Harley-Davidson.

It was Needham who returned fastest time of the day in winning the unlimited cc general class with a flying kilometre time of 22.2 seconds and a speed of 100.8 mph. In the car section of the competition a time and speed had been clocked by none other than world land-speed record contender Major Henry Seagrave with his famous straight-eight, two-litre Sunbeam. And so, after the interval, a special duel was arranged over the standing mile section of the course.

'Needham evidently realized that everything depended on getaway', reported *The Motor Cycle*, 'and at the fall of the flag the Brough literally leapt, and established a lead of several lengths. But as the red-jerseyed figure hurtled down the sands, the glistening vermilion racer with its white-clad driver swept up, and side by side they crossed the line, the verdict being that the motor cycle had won the day by half a wheel — a matter of a foot or so.'

Flushed with success, Needham and the Brough proved uncatchable in the 50-mile solo race, in the unlimited cc section of which (said the report) he had no serious challenger. However, he seems to have retried from sport at the end of the year — a press notice that he was marrying an American lady may offer a clue to the reason — and the Brough dropped out of sight until it was acquired fifty years later by David Eindhoven, and restored to original condition by specialist Tony Cripps.

In Brough-Superior production, the SS100 (the name indicative of its potential speed) was always the 1,000 cc overhead-valve twin, while the SS80 was the corresponding side-valve twin of the same size. Both were introduced at the 1924 Olympia Show, so the present machine was one of the first SS100 models to be built.

Unusually, it is fitted with a G. H. Jones-designed Wex carburettor of 'sliding door' type, and with Harley-Davidson front forks although George Brough and Harold Karslake had founded the Castle Fork Company in January 1925 to produce their own version of the Harley design under British patents.

Specification

Make Brough-Superior. **Model** SS100 Sprint. **Engine** 980 cc (85.7 × 85 mm bore and stroke) JAP Type KTOR overhead-valve vee-twin. **Power output** 50 bhp at 5,000 rpm. **Tyres** 3.00 × 21 in front and rear. **Frame** Brazed-lug tubular cradle. **Suspension** Harley-Davidson leading link and telescopic front forks. Rigid rear. **Weight** Not quoted. **Wheelbase** 56 in. **Manufacturer** George Brough, Haydn Road, Nottingham.

Above Specially built for sand-racing exponent Charles Needham, this 980 cc Brough-Superior was the winner in a race against Major Seagrave's famous Sunbeam straight-eight racing car. **Right** George Brough had already begun to manufacture his Castle copy of the Harley-Davidson front fork, but Needham's machine has genuine Harley forks. **Far right** Heart of the Brough-Superior SS100 is the 980 cc ohv JAP engine, which produces an impressive 50 bhp. **Below** Advertised as 'The Rolls-Royce of Motor Cycles', the Brough was the make to which every red-blooded motor cyclist aspired.

19

1921 499 cc BSA Senior TT

With military contracts suddenly chopped at the conclusion of World War 1, BSA were anxious to get back to motorcycle production in as big a way as possible. And what better way to get the assembly lines busy than by winning the Isle of Man Senior TT, the most prestigious race in the world at the time, with the world-wide publicity that would follow?

For a company that had not, so far, shown much racing prowess (there was but one BSA finisher in the 1913 Senior TT) the project was an audacious one, to say the least. But the BSA management was determined, and wartime contracts had left them with money to pour into the project — a small fortune, even by the standards of twenty years later. The objective was the 1920 Senior race, the first of the post-war meetings, but the design and competitions departments were not ready in time, and so the sights were retrained on the 1921 event.

The machine which emerged was completely unlike any BSA that had gone before. The engine was overhead valve, for a start (all previous BSAs had been side valve) with the valves mounted vertically in the rather skimpily-finned head and operated by rocker beams which were pressed upwards against a knife-edge cross-member. The engine was mounted in an inclined-forward position in a frame which, rather like that of the Cotton, featured tubes running directly from steering head to rear wheel spindle.

Novelties abounded, such as a cast-light-alloy one-into-two exhaust manifold and an extremely updraught double-drum carburettor of BSA's own manufacture. A large oil pump carried on the right of the oil tank was arranged to be operated by a pedal — though, in fact, there was already a brake pedal on that side.

Preliminary testing was carried out at Brooklands, and reports from that venue indicated that the BSAs were very fast indeed. But the concrete of Brooklands was a very different matter to the mountainous Isle of Man course, as would soon become clear.

No fewer than fourteen models were made ready for the TT assault, of which six would be the actual race machines, six would be for the practice period, and two would be spare. Troubles began almost as soon as the squad arrived at their Ramsey headquarters, for the machines wouldn't steer properly — a fault cured by a change of front-wheel size — and the patented valve clearance adjustment unscrewed itself in motion. Patented also was a slipper-type piston of cast-aluminium, which gave rise to frequent seizures.

Trying to work his foot-operated oil pump, Charlie North's foot slipped off the pedal and he broke an ankle. Carrying out carburation tests one morning, Gus Kuhn and Albert Wood collided, Kuhn damaging his ankle so badly that he was a non-starter.

Junior draughtsman on the project, and later BSA Chief Engineer, David Munro reflected many years later: 'If only the engine had been reliable, it would undoubtedly have been an outstanding model'. But reliability is what the Senior TT BSA lacked. Six machines did face the starter, but all six were eliminated by mechanical breakdown before the race was three laps old.

Specification

Make BSA. **Model** Senior TT. **Engine** 499 cc (85 × 88 mm bore and stroke) overhead-valve single. **Power output** Not quoted. **Tyres** 3.00 × 26 in (measured over tread) beaded-edge, front and rear. **Frame** Brazed-lug tubular diamond with twin front down tubes. **Suspension** BSA tubular girder front forks, undamped. Rigid rear. **Weight** 310 lb dry. **Wheelbase** 55 in. **Manufacturer** BSA Cycles Ltd, at their branch works at Redditch, Worcestershire.

Above First 'sloper' ever to emerge from BSA, the 1921 Senior TT model broke new ground in many directions — perhaps too much for its own good. **Right** Crude to modern eyes, braking comprised a fibre block operating in a dummy vee-belt pulley on each wheel. **Far right** The carburettor was BSA's own double-cylindrical type, mounted at an extraordinary updraught angle. Valves were vertical, the rocker arms pivoting on knife-edges. **Below** BSA's TT 'Grand Slam' was a disaster, all six machines retiring, mostly with piston failure. Thereafter, the BSA factory refused to countenance road racing.

1960 499 cc BSA Gold Star DBD34

To many an enthusiast's eye, BSA's svelte 'Clubman's Goldie' is *the* classic British bike of all time, and its lashings of chromium plating, all-alloy engine, swept-back exhaust pipe and twittering silencer, and clip-on handlebars evoke the 1950s in a way no other model can. Half-close your eyes, and you picture a smoke-filled coffee bar beside a by-pass, a juke-box playing an Elvis Presley record, leather bomber jackets with fringed sleeves...

There had been a Gold Star model in BSA's pre-World War 2 programme, but for all practical purposes the post-war Goldie can be considered as deriving from the basic 348 cc B31 iron-engine single of 1946. Development in those early post-war years was quite rapid, for next came the B32 competitions model then, at last, the 1948 B32 Gold Star which made use of a light-alloy cylinder barrel (with integral pushrod tower) and head.

What really pushed the Gold Star into the limelight was the coming of the ACU Clubman's TT in 1949, a race over the famous Isle of Man circuit for amateur riders mounted on stock road-going machinery. The winner proved to be Harold Clark in the 350 cc class, and from that point the Goldie never looked back. The first 499 cc Gold Star joined the family the same year, and although initially it was less successful on the race tracks than its smaller brother, the bigger model did gain its spurs in the International Six-Days Trial (held in Wales in September 1949) in which ten of the new 499 cc models earned gold medals.

The BSA factory was quick to take advantage of the early Clubman's TT success, and a whole series of go-faster items entered the catalogue, such as a TT carburettor, high-compression piston and cylinder head, high-lift cams, rearwardly-mounted footrests, and so on.

In the years which lay ahead, the Gold Star came to be so dominant in the Clubman's TT series that no other make had a look-in. (To take an example, there were 37 entries in the 1955 Junior Clubman's TT and 33 of those were on BSA Gold Stars!) But in the end, the overwhelming success of the Goldie led to its own downfall, for rather than run a one-horse — or to be more accurate, a one-breed-of-horse — race the ACU quietly killed off the Clubman's TT after 1956.

In passing it should be said that the Gold Star not only came in 348 and 499 cc forms, but in a number of guises — Clubman's, trials, and moto-cross — and indeed for a decade it carried the works teams to victory in cross-country events.

Back at the works, development had been continuing steadily until, in 1957, the ultimate 499 cc Clubman Gold Star was added to the range. This was the DBD34 (there was no equivalent 348 cc model this time, for the smaller machine was about to be dropped completely), listed in Clubman roadster and moto-cross versions only. The final specification embraced a redesigned cylinder head to accept a $1\frac{1}{2}$ in Amal GP carburettor, but the machine was becoming uneconomic to build and, to the lasting regret of BSA fans the world over, the Goldie died in mid-1963.

Specification

Make BSA. **Model** Gold Star DBD34. **Engine** 499 cc (85 × 88 mm bore and stroke) all-alloy overhead-valve single. **Power output** 40 bhp at 7,000 rpm. **Tyres** 3.00 × 21 in front, 3.25 × 19 in rear. **Frame** All-welded duplex tubular cradle. **Suspension** Oil-damped telescopic front forks. Swinging arm rear forks controlled by spring and hydraulic units. **Weight** 308 lb dry. **Wheelbase** 54 in. **Manufacturer** BSA Motor Cycles Ltd, Armoury Road, Small Heath, Birmingham 11.

Above In the days of the sports-roadster racing model, the BSA Gold Star was king of cafe society, the DBD34 model representing the ultimate of the breed. **Right** Clip-on handlebars and matched speedometer and rev-counter, were essential parts of the Goldie image. **Far right** The massively-finned light-alloy cylinder of the DBD illustrates how far the machine had come since the late 1940s. **Below** Known and loved by Gold Star fans everywhere were the swept-back Clubman exhaust system and the famous 'twittering' silencer. Acres of plating made Goldie the glamour girl of the BSA range.

1971 741 cc BSA Formula 750 Rocket Three

Formula 750 was a short-lived phenomena of the early to mid-1970s, which permitted machines originally constructed under the American Motorcycle Association's Daytona race rules, to race in Britain under Auto Cycle Union jurisdiction. Regulations acceptable to both organizations were thrashed out in February 1971 by AMA and ACU representatives and a race under F750 rules was added to the Isle of Man TT programme that year. With a crowded programme, however, the three-lap race would actually have to take place on the Saturday before TT Week proper and also, since the international governing body (the FIM) refused to ratify the formula, the F750 TT would have to be restricted to British riders only.

Basically, bikes built under Formula 750 were neither Grand Prix, nor 'production' (machines for officially recognized production racing had to be essentially as-per-catalogue). Instead, major items such as the engine and gearbox castings, the type of transmission and the number of gears had to be of production machine type, one hundred similar units having been made and sold to the public. That apart, it was a matter of 'anything goes', and the BSA-Triumph Group's F750 racers — the BSA Rocket Three and Triumph Trident were identical except for painting styles — were far removed from the roadster models from which they were initially derived.

Frames were of a compact, all-welded, twin-loop design produced by frame specialist Rob North of Nuneaton and the very characteristic racing fairing, with letter-box slot below the front racing number, was developed jointly by the Meriden race shop and Screen & Plastic, a glass-fibre company based at Redditch. In fact the frontal slot was an air intake for the oil radiator which was mounted in front of the machine's steering head; ducting at the rear of the radiator led hot air to outlets in the fairing sides. Another noticeable feature was a twin-disc-brake front wheel, fitting of which necessitated wider front forks than standard.

Three of the new machines, ridden by John Cooper, Ray Pickrell, and Percy Tait were included in the British squad which trounced the Americans in the first Eastertime three-meeting tournament staged at Brands Hatch, Mallory Park and Oulton Park. Over at Daytona, BSA-Triumph finished first and second, and there was further joy for the BSA Group when, in the first-ever F750 TT Tony Jefferies led Ray Pickrell across the line for another one-two victory. Tony's model was officially a Triumph (same thing, different colour) and his winning speed was 102.85 mph.

F750 racing was given FIM approval for 1972, and with the Norton team now joining in, the outlook for the Formula looked a little brighter. With one or two of the Continental organizers adding an F750 race to their meetings, the FIM were even able to stage a World Championship series. Again, a triple won the F750 TT — Ray Pickrell this time, on a 'Triumph' which had previously been raced by Mike Hailwood at Daytona as a 'BSA'. But time was fast running out for the BSA Group, and though several of the special racers would be seen on the circuits for some time to come — in particular, that ridden by John 'Mooneyes' Cooper — the works themselves had closed and development had come to a full stop.

Specification

Make BSA. **Model** Formula 750 Rocket Three. **Engine** 741 cc (67 × 70 mm bore and stroke) overhead-valve three-cylinder. **Power output** 84 bhp at 8,500 rpm. **Tyres** 3.25 × 19 in front, 4.10 × 19 in rear. **Frame** All-welded duplex tubular loop. **Suspension** Oil-damped telescopic front forks. Swinging-arm rear forks controlled by spring and hydraulic units. **Weight** Not quoted. **Wheelbase** 58 in. **Manufacturer** BSA Motor Cycles Ltd, Armoury Road, Small Heath, Birmingham 11.

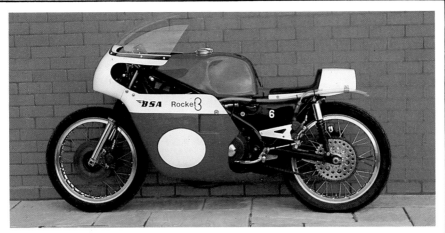

Above Looking very sedate by comparison with present-day race models, the Formula 750 Rocket Three could give an excellent account of itself. **Right** The 'letter box' slot in the frontal fairing gave air access to the engine oil cooler mounted in front of the steering head. **Far right** Tubes of the Rob North racing frame curve round the gearbox and make straight for the steering head. **Below** In the eyes of the British racing fans, this was possibly the most famous of all the BSA-group racing triples, for it was raced to victory on many occasions by John Cooper.

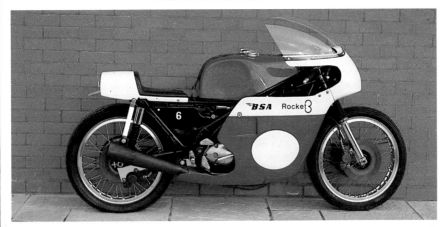

1972 499 cc Cheney-BSA John Banks Moto-Cross Special

John Banks was one of the riders who came into prominence in the late 1960s through the medium of television, for in that period both the BBC and commerical stations used moto-cross to fill what would otherwise be blank weekend screens during the winter months. By 1967, twice world champion Jeff Smith was tailing-off his globe-trotting career, preferring instead to contest home meetings, and so the Small Heath talent-spotters invited Banks to join the works team with a view to taking over where Smith left off in the world championship rounds.

Right nobly did John perform, too, for although he couldn't quite repeat Jeff Smith's feat, he did at least finish the 1968 world championships in second place, only one point behind Paul Friedrichs (CZ) of East Germany. In the following year, 1969, Banks again finished in runner-up spot, and a replica — or as near as may be — of the 499 cc works model was announced for production as the B50 Victor Grand Prix. Much of the competitions department's championship-chasing know-how had been built into the 38 bhp engine, and in consequence the B50 GP was probably the best four-stroke moto-cross model ever to enter series production.

But sad to say the skids were already under the whole BSA organization. The competitions department was closed as 1971 ran into autumn, and the works team was disbanded, with Jeff Smith emigrating to Canada to take up a post as development engineer with Bombardier (Can-Am), and John Banks signing up as a rider of Czechoslovakian-built CZ two-strokes.

Meanwhile, former works and international-class moto-cross rider Eric Cheney, an engineer of considerable ability, had been steadily making a reputation for himself as a frame manufacturer. Indeed, both Keith Hickman and Jerry Scott had contested the 1966 world moto-cross championships on BSA-powered Cheney models, and for the 1971 International Six-Days Trial he collaborated with the Triumph factory to produce a batch of Cheney-Triumphs for the British Trophy and Vase teamsters.

Basically a four-stroke man, John Banks had been unhappy with his CZ committment and so, for 1972, he gained the backing of Somerset-based motorcycle dealer Bernie Taylor, and commissioned a frame built in Reynolds 531 tubing from Eric Cheney, to which John fitted an ex-works BSA B50 Victor engine which had been given the typical 'Small Heath Comp Shop' treatment of a pineapple-finned cylinder (mainly a precaution against clogging of the fins by mud in a bad-weather event).

This, then, was the Cheney-BSA John Banks Special seen here, and with it John won the 500 cc British Moto-Cross Championships title. He campaigned the same machine in the world championship rounds, too, but with rather less success, having to retire in two of the events and finishing no higher than eleventh overall.

At this point, Eric Cheney could have benefitted from Banks' home championship victories by offering a Banks Replica, but he was frustrated by a shortage of BSA engines. However, in 1973 famous ISDT man Ken Heanes (who had won a gold medal in 1971 on a Cheney-Triumph) stepped in to negotiate an agreement for the release of BSA engines. Fitted into a Cheney frame, the machine was marketed for a while as the Heanes Thumper, but with the total collapse of BSA later the same year the venture folded.

Specification

Make Cheney-BSA. **Model** John Banks Moto-Cross Special. **Engine** BSA 499 cc (84 × 90 mm bore and stroke) overhead-valve single. **Power output** 38 bhp at 6,200 rpm. **Tyres** 3.00 × 20 in front, 4.00 × 18 in rear. **Frame** All-welded tubular cradle. **Suspension** Oil-damped telescopic front forks. Swinging-arm rear forks controlled by spring and hydraulic units. **Weight** 230 lb dry. **Wheelbase** 54 in. **Manufacturer** Eric Cheney Developments Ltd, Redfields Lane, Church Crookham, Aldershot, Hampshire.

Above Perhaps the ultimate in British four-stroke moto-cross machinery, the 1972 Cheney-BSA gave John Banks victory in the British Moto-Cross Championships. **Right** Eric Cheney's lightweight conical front hub helps keep front-end weight low. High, cross-braced handlebar suited John's riding style. **Far right** 'Pineapple' cylinder finning, a speciality of the BSA competitions department, prevented clogging in very muddy conditions. **Below** Rear wheel vertical travel seems infinitesimal by modern standards, but it appeared quite adequate for 1972 competition.

1929 497 cc Chater-Lea-JAP 'Copperknob'

You wouldn't think so to look at the model now, but the glittering all copper-plated racing machine which is one of the true treasures of the National Motorcycle Museum collection began life as an AA patrolman's hack. Or let's put it this way — the *frame* came from an AA patrol 545 cc side-valve Chater-Lea, but what Ben Bickell, a Brooklands star of the late 1920s and early 1930s, did to it was something else.

Later in this book you'll meet the totally nickel-plated Grindlay-Peerless campaigned at Brooklands by Bill Lacey. Well, it was that machine which gave Ben the idea of creating something special for himself. The Chater-Lea took shape in the winter of 1928–29 in the garage at Highgate, London, run by brothers Joe and Ben Bickell, and though the main frame diamond of the AA bike was retained (even to the sidecar mounting lug on the front down tube), it now sported Druid ES-type (Enclosed Spring) racing front forks in which the central spring was encased in a telescopic tube with controllable friction damping.

In place of the humdrum 545 cc side-valve engine there was now a very potent 497 cc JAP. Additional strengthening tubes ran from the region of the rear spindle to the massive engine rear mounting plates, the only brake was at the rear and worked by a very rear-set pedal and short rod, mudguards were non-existent and the seating arrangement was a completely unsprung saddle.

But what really took the spectators' eyes as Ben wheeled out the machine for its racing debut, at the opening Brooklands meeting of the 1929 season, was that it was copper plated from stem to stern. Just to complete the ensemble, he had even copper plated his helmet! Indeed, when Ben Bickell first donned that helmet in the paddock, other riders greeted him with cries of 'Hello, Copperknob'. And though the nickname was applied to Ben himself, somehow it became transferred to his machine, which was known as Copperknob thereafter.

In that first 1929 outing, Ben and the Chater-Lea-JAP had a terrific tussle with Les Archer, senior, on a New Imperial, and it was Archer who gained the flag. But from then on, wins came thick and fast with, each winter, Joe and Ben Bickell managing to extract just a little more urge. A particularly interesting meeting in 1931 was sponsored by the JAP factory, and restricted to riders of machines powered by 500 cc JAP engines. For this season Ben had a new power plant — in fact one of the then-new JAP speedway engines, skimpy finning and all; but since he was running on alcohol anyway, minimal finning was no problem.

Bickell led the race throughout, to win at an average speed of 93.97 mph. But after the 1932 season, his outings on Copperknob were less frequent because he had now switched his main effort to Ariels. Sadly, Ben was killed on an Ariel in the 1936 Ulster Grand Prix and Copperknob disappeared from view when the Bickell Brothers garage was sold. However, it hadn't travelled far, and was rediscovered in 1950 in Johnny Lock's garage in Edmonton. It then passed through several hands, until it was acquired by Sid King in the 1960s in a totally dismantled state.

Gradually the model arose from the boxes of bits, missing items were remade or substituted, and after a deal of work 'Copperknob' made a triumphant return to Brooklands at one of the reunion meetings held at the now defunct track.

Specification

Make Chater-Lea. **Model** Special. **Engine** 497 cc (80 × 99 mm bore and stroke) JAP overhead-valve single. **Power output** Not quoted. **Tyres** 3.00 × 20 in front, 3.25 × 20 in rear. **Frame** Brazed-lug tubular diamond, copper plated. **Suspension** Druid Type ES girder front forks, with friction damper. Rigid rear. **Weight** Not quoted. **Wheelbase** 54.5 in. **Manufacturer** (frame) Chater-Lea Manufacturing Co Ltd, Letchworth Garden City, Hertfordshire.

Above Completely copper-plated from stem to stern, Ben Bickell's Chater-Lea was immediately recognizable in a Brooklands race. **Right** Front forks are Druid ES type, the initials signifying 'Enclosed Spring'. **Far right** Power unit is an early-pattern speedway JAP. Cylinder finning is minimal, but was not required anyway, because 'Copperknob' always ran on an alcohol fuel. **Below** Though the Bickell Special is very obviously a track bike, even to the obligatory 'Brooklands Can' silencer, it began life as an AA road patrol model. The polished finish permitted incipient metal-fatigue cracks to be spotted quickly.

1927 438 cc Cotton-Blackburne Senior TT

Rumours that the Blackburne engine factory had been at work on something very hush-hush through the 1926–27 winter were confirmed when, at one of the early-spring Brooklands meetings, Paddy Johnston appeared with a very unusual overhead-camshaft engine stowed into the frame of a Zenith. However, the Zenith was merely fortuitous, and *Motor Cycling* for 25 May 1927 revealed that in fact Cotton would be contesting all three TT classes, using the new design of engine in 248 cc (60 × 88 mm), 348 cc (71 × 88 mm) and 438 cc (76 × 96.6 mm) sizes.

An odd capacity, that Senior TT engine? Well, yes, but the Blackburne people explained it like this: 'The decision to make the Senior engine of the size given has been governed by a variety of reasons, one of which is that experience in the past has proved that the Junior engines have so nearly approached the Seniors in the matter of performance that the sacrifice of a few cubic centimetres capacity is not considered to be of vital importance'.

The three engines were visually very much alike, even to using identical crankcase castings, and the majority of parts were interchangeable. There was a single overhead camshaft (on which ran duralumin rockers), but instead of using a shaft-and-bevel drive, Blackburne employed a vertical shaft with a skew gear at each end. The skew gear on the half-time shaft was used, also, to drive by forward-facing horizontal shaft an ML magneto.

Dry-sump lubrication was an unexpected refinement in 1927, and a duplex plunger-type pump, located at the base of the vertical cam-drive shaft, was arranged to supply oil under pressure to both the big-end bearing and, by way of the hollow vertical shaft, to the cambox.

It has to be said that the engine was a rather ungainly lump, and though the Cotton factory did their best to adhere to the triangulated frame structure which had served them so well thus far, they had to make an offset frame in which the engine hung out to the right, and that in turn meant bending some of the frame tubes to suit. Notable also was the use of very large rear engine/gearbox mounting plates which replaced the normal seat pillar.

Other details embraced a steering head which employed a taper roller bearing at the lower end, but a thrust race at the top — and operation of *both* brakes by pedal. Previous Cottons had employed a handsome tapered fuel tank inserted between the frame top rails, but the height of the overhead-camshaft engine precluded that and, instead, there was a most peculiar flat-sided tank which sat over the top rails in a horizontal plane.

Paddy Johnston, Cotton's No 1 works rider at the time, was detailed to ride the one-and-only Senior TT Cotton Blackburne (the other works Cotton in the same event, ridden by Harry Brockbank, employed a pushrod vee-twin engine), but though Paddy finished fifth in the Junior TT, he crashed at the Bungalow while lying a nicely-placed fourth in the 250 cc Lightweight, damaging his ribs.

That left the Cotton team in something of a hole, but into the breach stepped Bill Colgan, an Irish Cotton regular, who fortunately had qualified as a reserve. However, Bill was never anywhere in the picture, and the Cotton dropped out with unspecified mechanical trouble on the sixth of the seven laps, and was never seen on the island again.

Specification

Make Cotton. **Model** Senior TT. **Engine** Blackburne 438 cc (76 × 96.8 mm bore and stroke) overhead-camshaft single. **Power output** Not quoted. **Tyres** 27 × 2.75 in (21 × 2¾ in) front and rear. **Frame** Cotton patented triangulated construction, brazed and lugged. **Suspension** Webb girder front forks, with friction dampers. Rigid rear. **Weight** 340 lb. **Wheelbase** 54 in. **Manufacturer** Cotton Motors, Vulcan Works, Quay Street, Gloucester.

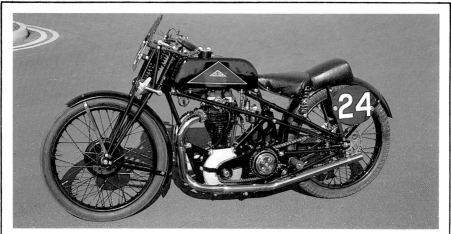

Above A long way from the usual Cotton standards of beauty, the 1927 Senior TT model was really a matter of expediency. **Right** Width of the awkwardly placed fuel tank, which completely envelopes the oil tank, is evident in this frontal view. **Far right** Use of skew gearing in the overhead-camshaft drive results in a most unusual appearance. Note also the forwardly-placed magneto. **Below** Because the engine was off-centre to the right, the celebrated Cotton triangulated frame had to be modified, with dire consequences upon the steering.

1928 494 cc Douglas DT5

Although the origins of speedway (or dirt-track as it was known at first) lay in America, the sport is generally acknowledged to have taken on recognizable shape at a meeting organized by Johnnie Hoskins in 1926 at the West Maitland Electric Light Carnival in Australia. That led to other Australian dirt-track events, and eventually word spread to Britain of this wonderfully exciting new form of motorcycle racing.

The first officially organized meeting in England took place under ACU licence at High Beech, an athletic track in the depths of Epping Forest, on 19 February 1928. Of course local riders had no real idea of how to tackle the short, cinder-covered oval, but to ride at that opening event came two Australians with experience of dirt racing 'down under'. They were Keith McKay and Billy Galloway, both mounted on long and low Model RA Douglas flat twins, virtually replicas of the Douglas TT model though with the brakes disconnected.

The art of riding the 'dirt Duggie' was to forget about brakes and drive purely on the throttle, flinging the machine broadside into the bends and throwing up a wave of black cinders. It was sheer spectacle, aided by the unsilenced roar of the twin-cylinder engine. Add the drama of racing under floodlights (another element of speedway racing which arrived after the first few months), and the magic became almost tangible.

From High Beech, dirt-track spread the length and breadth of England, and tracks sprang up in all the likely — and a few unlikely — localities. More and more Aussies arrived to show their skill, and Douglas factory got to work to devise a machine specifically for the new sport. In essence, it comprised the front section of an RA frame married to the rear part of the earlier OB design. The first prototype was loaned to New Zealand ace Stewie St George for a meeting at Manchester. He despatched a telegram to the Bristol firm immediately after the event. 'Motor and frame perfect', it ran. 'Won everything. St George.'

Elated, the Douglas people put the machine into production immediately as the 494 cc Model DT5 (there was also a 600 cc version, the DT6). The standard engine was claimed to produce 27 bhp, but for an extra £10 a customer could order a factory-tuned engine capable of turning out 32 bhp, prepared and assembled at the works by Rex Judd and Freddie Dixon, no less.

Peak year for production was 1929, when no fewer than 1,300 dirt-track models were sold, and the model was to remain in the catalogue until 1932. That year the price of the 494 cc model had come down with a bump from the original £85 to £75, but that failed to halt the slide in sales, and at the end of the 1932 season Douglas bowed out of the speedway field. The reason was that for all the noise and spectacle of the Duggie, the arrival of short-wheelbase singles from Rudge and JAP proved that a rider could corner in a less showy fashion — and reach the finish line first.

Some of the unsold speedway Douglas models were converted to road specification and sold off to sporty lads. Others drifted down into grass-track racing and eventual oblivion, but the impact of the Douglas on speedway will never be forgotten.

Specification

Make Douglas. **Model** DT5. **Engine** 494 cc (62.25 × 82 mm bore and stroke) overhead-valve horizontally opposed twin. **Power output** 27 bhp at 5,000 rpm. **Tyres** 28 × 2.5 in beaded-edge front and rear. **Frame** Brazed-lug tubular duplex cradle. **Suspension** Girder front forks with friction dampers. Rigid rear. **Weight** Not quoted. **Wheelbase** 57.5 in. **Manufacturer** Douglas Motors Ltd, Hanham Road, Kingswood, Bristol.

Above Undoubted star of Britain's early dirt tracks, the long and low flat-twin Douglas necessitated a leg-trailing riding style. **Right** Far removed from the speedway bikes of today, the 'dirt Duggie' was in fact derived from a road racing model. **Far right** In 1928, track bikes still had hand-change gearboxes; the knee hook was a necessary aid to broadsiding on cinders. **Below** Centre of gravity of the Douglas was exceptionally low, contributing greatly to its spectacular cornering, but by the early 1930s it was being eclipsed by the quicker but less flamboyant singles.

1932 498 cc Excelsior-JAP B14 Isle of Man TT

The long-established Excelsior concern had been associated with road and track racing ever since the dawn of motorcycling and, making use of proprietary engines (usually by J. A. Prestwich, of London) the marque established an enviable record both on the Isle of Man — where Syd Crabtree, on an Excelsior-JAP, won the 1929 Lightweight TT at record speed — and at Brooklands where they were raced by such notabilities as Eric Fernihough, Chris Staniland and Tony Worters.

Excelsior's B14 model was a series-production racer which entered the factory's programme late in 1931 and remained until 1933. It was described as the '500 cc special Isle of Man TT model', and the makers claimed that it had a frame identical to that used by the firm's own 1931 TT team, the whole machine being the outcome of wide racing experience. The 498 cc JAP engine was specially tuned to achieve 100 mph, and it drove through a three-speed Burman gearbox.

In Excelsior publicity material, the makers pointed to wins in the South African TT, European Grand Prix, Belgian Grand Prix and Swedish TT; but they kept rather quiet about the Isle of Man TT, the 1931 Senior race entries for which had been Charlie Dodson and Syd Crabtree.

Describing the 1931 TT machines, *The Motor Cycle* commented: 'Last year's TT Excelsiors were very light, owing to careful detail design, and for the forthcoming races are likely to be even lighter. A considerable saving has been brought about by the use of Elektron castings; also, heavy forged pedals have given way to lighter but equally substantial pressings. The wheel hubs are carefully machined from forgings, and aluminium is employed for the brake shoes. Some savings had also been made in the way of the frame by modifications to the lower part of the loop.'

J. A. Prestwich had played their part, too, by presenting a redesigned 498 cc engine weighing only 67 lb, as against the 86 lb of its predecessor. Internally there were lighter flywheels, polished all over, and the big-end ran on a double-row, positively lubricated roller bearing.

In the actual race... 'Charlie Dodson was the first of the real aces to get away, and his fierce JAP spluttered like a baby two-stroke for some yards before it condescended to produce its full bass roar', but all was far from well and he reached no further than Quarter Bridge before stopping to change the sparking plug. He got going again, but was never anywhere in the hunt, and he dropped out on the sixth lap. Meanwhile, team mate Syd Crabtree did work up to eleventh place then he, too, packed in.

However, there was rather better luck elsewhere, and Eric Fernihough took his 498 cc Excelsior-JAP to victory at Gatwick Sprint, while Bill Kitchen (later to make his mark as Wembley Speedway captain) swept all before him on a similar model at Southport Sands.

Using what appeared to be as-per-catalogue Model B14 racers, Crabtree and Dodson were again the official works entries in the 1932 Senior TT, and though Crabtree lasted no more than one lap, Dodson did finish in a respectable fifth place. He was, said *Motor Cycling*, 'a model of consistent riding, lacking only in utter maximum speed'. Still, a 77.26 mph average for the race wasn't exactly hanging about, and the Excelsior was certainly the highest-placed of the various JAP-engined entries.

Above The Excelsior factory marketed their B14 racer as being 'an exact replica of our own TT team machines'. A speed of 100 mph was claimed. **Right** Good handling was always an Excelsior virtue, in which the Webb girder-type front forks played a part. **Far right** This was the last year in which the firm would rely on JAP racing engines, for their own 'Mechanical Marvel' was already on the drawing board. **Below** The B14 Excelsior-JAP was particularly successful in overseas racing, but Isle of Man performance was disappointing, both 1932 Senior TT entries retiring.

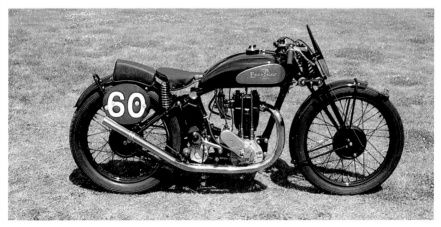

1936 349 cc Excelsior Manxman FR12

One of the oldest names — if not the oldest — in the British motorcycle industry, Excelsior began in 1874 by building penny-farthing cycles, but in the late 1890s they were already producing track-racing motorcycles powered by MMC engines and their works-supported rider Sam Wright was one of the first stars of the game. Nevertheless, Excelsior were something of a Jekyll-and-Hyde outfit, and for all their considerable racing reputation throughout the years, the company earned its daily bread from the manufacture of cheap and cheerful two-stroke utility models.

Not until just before World War 2 did the factory possess any engine-manufacturing facilities, and so their pre-war racing programme had perforce to rely on proprietary engines such as JAP, or on engines specially designed and built on their behalf by some outside concern.

One such unit was the 250 cc 'Mechanical Marvel' of 1933, designed exclusively for Excelsior by Ike Hatch of the Blackburne company, and manufactured at the Blackburne plant near Brooklands. It was successful in that an Excelsior 'Mechanical Marvel' piloted by Syd Gleave won the Lightweight TT of that year. However, it was a finicky engine to work on, and to keep in racing tune, and Eric Walker of Excelsiors was looking for something which could not only be raced, but could form the basis of a production model.

So he and Hatch tried again in 1935, and the outcome was a rugged-looking overhead-camshaft engine with shaft-and-bevel drive to the camshaft. This was one of the most successful racing designs of all time and, as the Excelsior Manxman, was to gain a wholesome reputation for high-speed reliability.

No better proof can be found than by perusing the results of the 1939 Lightweight TT. Faced with the might of Germany's blown DKW two-strokes, the Excelsiors didn't win the race — but their finishers included second, third, fourth, fifth, sixth, seventh and ninth places!

The Excelsior factory itself had a formidable race team led by Tyrell Smith, and they promised customers that the production Manxman race models were 'genuine racing machines, not replicas'. Each was 'hand built and tested by our racing and experimental department', and even the tyres were (according to the Manxman sales brochure) 'fitted by the Dunlop race mechanics'. The machine was listed in 250, 350 and 500 cc sizes, and though primarily intended for road circuits it could be built to special order with a grass-track racing specification. Additionally, road-going sports versions of each were produced, equipped with full Miller Dynamag lighting and a conventional riding position.

The Blackburne factory, which had been building the engines to Excelsior order, closed down in 1937 but Manxman production carried on unchecked (there was even a 1940 wartime sales brochure, though it is doubtful if any models were built that year), the reason being that the Excelsior factory had begun to machine some of the parts themselves, the rest being entrusted to former car manufacturer, Beans Industries.

Our example, the 1936 Model FR12 (the 'R' signifying 'race specification') features bronze cylinder head, racing cams and valves, high-compression piston and Amal TT carburettor tuned for a 50/50 benzol mixture, close-ratio four-speed gearbox, TT tank, and rear-set footrests and controls. It really looked the part — and in this case looks were not deceptive.

Specification

Make Excelsior. **Model** Manxman FR12. **Engine** 349 cc (75 × 79 mm bore and stroke) single overhead-camshaft single. **Power output** 24 bhp at 6,000 rpm. **Tyres** 3.00 × 21 in front, 3.25 × 20 in rear. **Frame** Brazed-lug tubular with forged steel cradle. **Suspension** Webb racing girder front forks. Rigid rear. **Weight** 310 lb dry. **Wheelbase** 54 in. **Manufacturer** Excelsior Motor Co. Ltd, Kings Road, Tyseley, Birmingham 11.

Above The Birmingham-based Excelsior factory earned most of its corn in the less-than-glamorous commuter lightweight field — but when they did build a road-racer, the makers did it in style! The superlative Manxman employed much of the engineering of the TT-winning 'Mechanical Marvel'. **Right** Even the front tyre (according to Excelsior publicity) was 'fitted by the Dunlop race mechanics'! **Far right** A particularly sturdy shaft-and-bevel assembly took the drive to the overhead camshaft and a bronze cylinder head was fitted. **Below** Excelsior resumed production following World War 2 — but not, alas, of the Manxman.

1962 249 cc Francis-Barnett Trials 85

Long before the world of trials was conquered by the Spanish Armada of Bultaco, Montesa and Osso two-strokes, the big four-strokes that had ruled the roost for so many years were already having to fight off a formidable challenge from British lightweights powered by Villiers engines; there were Dot, Norman and James, and from Coventry there was the elegant Francis-Barnett. Formed as long ago as 1919, Francis-Barnett had been taken into the Associated Motor Cycles combine in mid-1947, although production continued at the little factory in the shadow of the remains of the bomb-damaged Coventry Cathedral for a number of years thereafter, under the eye of Eric Barnett, son of one of the founders of the concern.

Trials machines entered the range in 1952 in 125 and 197 cc sizes, using competitions versions of Villiers engines in suitably modified roadster frames with stiffened front forks and increased ground clearance. At first, no rear suspension was provided (because the diehard trials rider didn't want it) but by 1954 swinging-arm springing had become accepted wear.

The factory supported a full trials team in all the major events, and gradually the production version of the trials Fanny-B grew to be a very purposeful little bike indeed with a compact loop-type frame, and a brief rear sub-frame to carry the upper mounting of the rear shock units and the skimpy little Dunlop rubber saddle.

Meanwhile the parent AMC group had been developing a series of two-stroke engines of their own manufacture, and from 1958 the Francis-Barnett Trials 83 had to discard its Villiers power plant and adopt the 249 cc AMC single, like it or not. This particular machine was actually derived from the firm's works scramblers and featured an almost identical loop frame with Girling rear suspension units and a Norton telescopic front fork with two-way hydraulic damping. The Plumstead-made AMC engine unit incorporated a wide-ratio four-speed gear cluster, and the exhaust system was carried inboard of the right-hand rear sub-frame member and damper unit, where it would be less susceptible to damage.

The Trials 83 was campaigned in all the major British events, and in the autumn of 1958 a trio comprising competitions manager Ernie Smith and the brothers Triss and Bryan Sharp, entered for the International Six-Days Trial, held that year in Bavaria. All three finished, collecting the very respectable total of two gold medals and one bronze.

However, very little further development of the trials mount was carried on thereafter, for the AMC group as a whole was running into financial difficulties (though Francis-Barnett itself was still profitable). Built in 1962, the cobby little Trials 85 displayed at the National Motocycle Museum represents the final version of the AMC-powered model, for within a few months the AMC would be dropped and, instead, the power plant would be the well-liked 246 cc Villiers Mark 32A. But it represents also the end of Fanny-B production in Coventry, for as a drastic economy measure the works were closed down late in 1962. For the few years that remained to the group, Francis-Barnett and James were to share the James factory at Greet, Birmingham. Already there was a cuckoo in the nest, for another part of the same works had been let — to Suzuki (GB) Ltd who were beginning to import models from Japan.

Specification

Make Francis-Barnett. **Model** Trials 85. **Engine** 249 cc (66 × 73 mm bore and stroke) AMC two-stroke single. **Power output** 12 bhp at 5,000 rpm. **Tyres** 2.75 × 21 in front, 4.00 × 19 in rear. **Frame** All-welded single tubular loop. **Suspension** Norton hydraulically-damped telescopic front forks. Swinging-arm rear forks controlled by spring and hydraulic units. **Weight** 273 lb dry. **Wheelbase** 52.75 in. **Manufacturer** Francis & Barnett Ltd, Lower Ford Street, Coventry, Warwickshire.

Above Handsome in green and silver, the little Francis-Barnett typified the lighter British trials mount of the 1950s and 1960s. **Right** Francis-Barnett were part of the AMC combine, and so were able to make use of the greatly-respected Norton oil-damped front forks. **Far right** Though based on the Vincent Piatti-designed roadster engine, the trials unit featured a special cylinder head, and a wide-ratio four-speed gearbox. **Below** 1962 was the final year for Francis-Barnett at their original Coventry home, before moving to the James factory at Birmingham.

1955 197 cc Greeves 20T Trials

Pretty it certainly is, in its livery of Moorland Blue and polished light-alloy; but the regrettable fact is that in the 1955 Model 20T Trials, the Greeves factory had not quite got things right. Still, it was their first-ever attempt at a produciton trials model, and they were fast learners; throughout that season they would be making gradual improvements to their own development machines — increased steering lock, sealed ball-bearing wheel hubs (instead of the plain bronze bushes used, rather incredibly, on the machine pictured here), footrests moved further to the rear, and so on.

For 1956, then, the Greeves 20T would be a very different machine. It would have the advantage of the new Mark 9E (instead of 8E) Villiers engine-gear unit, Girling shock absorbers at the rear instead of rubber-in-torsion units, and a shorter wheelbase. But that was in the 'coming shortly' province, and for the moment the trials-riding public were rather wary of the new Greeves.

Mainly, they were wary of the unusual frame construction, which employed a cast-light-alloy beam (which encompassed the steering head also) as the front-down member, with further light-alloy castings as a cradle for the power unit. I mean to say! Alloy! Dead fragile, surely? And on a trials model, meant to be bashed about over rocks?

Well, in fact it was a particularly tough form of light-alloy, and at the Earls Court Motor Cycle Show the Greeves people displayed a very bent and mangled frame beam, as proof of just how much punishment the material would stand without fracturing. The use of light alloy reflected the company's establishment of their own aluminium foundry, for the truth was that Greeves motorcycles were an offshoot of the Invacar Company, manufacturers of powered invalid carriages which employed a number of cast-light-alloy parts. Moreover, Invacar used rubber-in-torsion suspension on the invalid chairs, and it was for this reason that similar units were featured at front and rear of the motorcycle. At the rear the rubber units (with handwheel adjustment of the degree of damping) were housed in the loops of the rear sub-frame and operated by rods from the rear pivoted fork. At the front they were located at the base of the fork stanchions, and controlled the short leading-link forks (a tubular loop passing round the back of the front tyre ensured that there would be no twisting of the wheel spindle).

Greeves were latecomers to the world of trials, for the two-stroke invasion had been gradually ousting the big four-strokes for the past several years. For example, there were no fewer than 78 assorted machines powered by Villiers two-stroke engines in the 1955 Scottish Six-Days Trial. Only one of those was a Greeves, surrounded by hordes of Dots, Jameses, Normans, and whatever. The lone 20T was ridden by Irish entry Bill Hutton, and it is pleasing to report that Bill finished the week with a first-class award to his credit.

That, at least, must have been an encouragement to the ambitious and enthusiastic little Greeves concern. But as time would prove, there would be great days ahead for Greeves (they would even be asked, as we shall soon see, to provide mounts for Britain's ISDT squad).

Specification

Make Greeves. **Model** 20T Trials. **Engine** Villiers 197 cc (59 × 72 mm bore and stroke) Mark 9E two-stroke single. **Power output** 8.4 bhp at 4,000 rpm. **Tyres** 2.75 × 21 in front, 4.00 × 18 in rear. **Frame** Composite construction of cast light-alloy and tubular steel. **Suspension** Leading-link front forks with rubber-in-torsion springing medium. Swinging arm rear forks controlled by rubber-in-torsion units. **Weight** 228 lb dry. **Wheelbase** 52 in. **Manufacturer** Greeves Motor Cycles (Invacar Ltd), Church Street, Thundersley, Essex.

Above The 1955 Model 20T was the little Greeves factory's first venture into commercial production of a trials machine. The light-alloy frame beam is very evident, as is the rubber-in-torsion springing at front and rear. **Right** In later years, slim hydraulic damper units would be concealed within the front fork legs, but the 1955 suspension was friction-damped. **Far right** Engine is the familiar 197 cc Villiers with cast-iron barrel; in time, Greeves would produce their own light-alloy barrel. **Below** Unusual in appearance, the Greeves was craggy but endearing, with a character all its own.

1963 246 cc Greeves ISDT Special

First instituted in 1913, the International Six-Days Trial had long been recognized as the toughest competition any motorcycle has ever had to tackle (the same contest continues today, but with a change of name, for now it is termed the International Six-Days Enduro) but Britain's teams for the Trophy and Vase sections of the event had traditionally used heavy four-stroke machines — basically roadster models, but given a modicum of road-race tuning in view of the high speed schedules that had to be maintained between checkpoints and the road-circuit speed trial which always concluded the trial.

For 1963, however, there was a change. Lighter two-stroke machines had been making considerable headway in national trials and international moto-cross, with Greeves foremost among the smaller British factories. Such was their reputation, indeed, that when the Auto Cycle Union broke with tradition and decided to include a couple of two-strokes in the ISDT squad (even though they were to be in the Vase B team, not the prestigious Trophy quintet), it was to Greeves that they turned.

That year the 'International' was to be held in the Czechoslovakian mountains around Spindleruv-Mlyn, 90 miles to the north-east of Prague. Since they were producing two bikes for the official British ACU entry, the Greeves firm decided they may as well build another and so give themselves a crack at the manufacturers' team award. Bryan and Triss Sharp (sons of pre-war Crystal Palace speedway ace, Triss Sharp, senior) were the two Vase B men and, with Peter Stirland, they would form the factory trio.

Derived from the Greeves Model 24MDS scrambler, the machines employed the familiar cast-light-alloy frame beam construction, with leading-link Greeves front forks and swinging-arm rear suspension using rectangular-section fork arms. Bottom-end assembly of the engine was basically the 246 cc Villiers Mark 36A but with a special Alpha full-circle crankshaft assembly, on top of which sat a square-finned light-alloy barrel and head of Greeves own manufacture, the whole engine and gearbox unit being finished in heat-dissipating matt black paint.

Ignition was by conventional Villiers flywheel magneto, but for use in emergencies a secondary system was provided, with a reserve ignition coil and condenser (mounted under the fuel tank) which could be energized from the lighting coil of the flywheel magneto.

Yet for all the meticulous pre-trial preparation, the British effort was doomed. After machines had been checked in at trial headquarters, they had to stand in the open all night until the official start time next morning, with penalty points for those whose mounts failed to start within the permitted three minutes. Sadly, one of those whose bikes were reluctant starters was Triss Sharp, riding as No 80 on the machine pictured here. But there was far worse to come, for when he did get going it was to travel but five miles before retiring altogether with a seized big-end bearing.

His brother Bryan and Peter Stirland, on the other two works-prepared 246 cc Greeves models finished the week triumphantly with a gold medal apiece. Stirland, in fact, made the best performance of the entire British entry, to finish ninth among the 'two-fifties'; but that was poor consolation for the loss of the greater glory. The Sharp brothers and their Greeves machines were again included in the ISDT squad for 1964, but both retired.

Specification

Make Greeves. **Model** ISDT Special. **Engine** 246 cc (66 × 72 mm bore and stroke) Villiers two-stroke single with Alpha and Greeves modifications. **Power output** 22 bhp at 6,000 rpm. **Tyres** 2.75 × 19 in front, 4.00 × 18 in rear. **Frame** Composite cast-light-alloy and steel tube. **Suspension** Short-leading-link front forks with spring and hydraulic units within fork stanchions. Swinging-arm rear forks controlled by spring and hydraulic units. **Weight** 200 lb dry. **Wheelbase** 52 in. **Manufacturer** Greeves Motor Cycles, Church Road, Thundersley, Essex.

Above Britain had traditionally relied on heavy four-stroke models for the International Six-Days Trial team riders, but in 1963 came a breakthrough when Greeves two-strokes were included for the first time. **Right** For many years, the light-alloy frame beam, and rubber-in-torsion front fork springing, were Greeves specialities. **Far right** The engine is a hybrid, employing Villiers crankcases, Alpha crankshaft, and Greeves cylinder barrel and head. **Below** Ridden by Britain's Silver Vase teamster, Triss Sharp, 'No 80' failed to finish the trial, but paved the way for subsequent participation.

1928 490 cc Grindlay-Peerless-JAP Bill Lacey Special

Not for nothing was Brooklands racing man C. W. G. (Bill) Lacey known to track habitués as 'Nickel Plate' Lacey, for he took pride in bringing his machines to the starting grid with not even a speck of dust to mar their state of perfection. Almost certainly the model which represents the very pinnacle of Bill Lacey's art is the totally nickel-plated Grindlay-Peerless with which, on 1 August 1928, he became the first Briton to average 100 mph for one hour, using a 500 cc bike on British soil.

The ton-in-the-hour had been achieved before, by Claude Temple in 1925 on a 996 cc OEC-Temple, but to hit that target he had had to stage his run at Montlhery Autodrome, outside Paris. That was when the weekly magazine, *The Motor Cycle,* came forward with a magnificent silver cup for he who would do the trick on a bike of half the engine capacity and, what's more, do it in Britain.

Indeed there was only one British venue where such an attempt could be made — the bumpy concrete bowl of Brooklands, near Weybridge, Surrey — and even then the powerful local anti-noise lobby insisted that all machines circulating the track must be equipped with silencers (known to all and sundry as 'Brooklands cans').

There was no lack of volunteers to accept the challenge, but the magic ton-hour remained out of reach until, on that Wednesday evening in 1928, Lacey wheeled his gleaming Grindlay on to the track, checked with the offical timekeeper, then gave it the gun. 'At the end of one of the most hectic hours he can ever have known', reported *The Motor Cycle* in the following week's issue, 'Lacey stepped off his still almost spotless Grindlay-Peerless, and smiled broadly and happily...' Indeed, he had averaged 103.3 mph for the hour, and the silver cup was rightly his.

One of the smallest of British motorcycle factories, Grindlay (Coventry) Ltd were, among other things, sidecar manufacturers and general engineers. They were also, as was very obvious, skilled builders of racing frames. The engines they fitted were produced by J. A. Prestwich of London, though it must be said that Bill Lacey's record-breaking motor was something exceptional for Bill himself had modified it by fitting rocker gear, rocker-box castings, pushrod tubes and cams of his own design and make.

Why nickel-plate the frame and tank? For the very practical reason that a plated component is easier to keep clean and, in consequence, a possible metal-fatigue crack can be spotted more readily. Cashing in on the hundred-in-the-hour record, Grindlay-Peerless built half a dozen Lacey Replica models (though with less rorty engines) and each was sold with a certificate that the machine had lapped Brooklands at 100 mph with Bill in the saddle.

The original record-breaker passed out of Lacey's hands, at first to Francis Beart (who broke the Brooklands Test Hill record on it) then to Eric Fernihough, who hired it out to aspiring riders who wanted to earn the little Brooklands Gold Star lapel badge awarded to those who lapped the track at 100 mph in a BMCRC race. With the outbreak of war the famous model dropped out of sight, and didn't surface again until it was found, in 1971, in a shed owned by a one-time associate of the late Eric Fernihough. The original race engine had been returned to JAP after the record run, and the engine now fitted is a similar one, on which the special Bill Lacey parts have been faithfully reproduced.

Specification

Make Grindlay-Peerless. **Model** Bill Lacey Special. **Engine** JAP 490 cc (80 × 90 mm bore and stroke) Type JOR overhead-valve single. **Power output** Not quoted. **Tyres** 3.00 × 21 in front and rear. **Frame** Brazed-lug tubular diamond, nickel plated. **Suspension** Brampton girder front forks, with patented progressive-action friction dampers. Rigid rear. **Weight** 250 lb. **Wheelbase** 53.25 in. **Manufacturer** Grindlay (Coventry) Ltd, Shakleton Road, Spon End, Coventry.

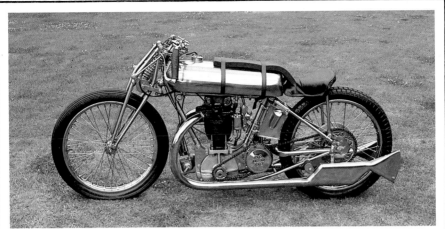

Above One of the most eye-catching machines ever to appear at the Brooklands circuit, Bill Lacey's nickel-plated Grindlay-Peerless was the first all-British bike to pack 100 miles into the hour on British soil. **Right** Special Brampton girder front forks incorporate progressive friction damping at each side. **Far right** Though the engine was JAP factory property, Lacey embodied many individual touches, including his own design of rocker gear. **Below** In the 1930s, the famous Grindlay-Peerless was hired out to those who wanted to lap Brooklands at the magic 100 mph.

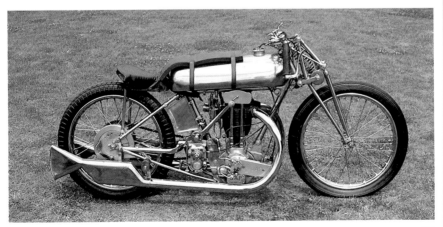

1914 496 cc
Matchless Works TT

Not until the mid-1920s did H. Collier & Sons Ltd, the famous manufacturers of Matchless motorcycles, take up production of their own engines. In earlier days, when the brothers Charlie and Harry Collier raced turn-of-the-century Matchless models on the cycle stadia around London, their mounts were essentially strengthened bicycle frames on which were hung primitive MMC engines, but as motorcycle technology improved, so JAP and MAG power units were employed.

Matchless had supported the Isle of Man TT Races from the very beginning, and it is a matter of history that Charlie Collier, on a JAP-engined model, won the single-cylinder class of the first TT meeting in 1907. Later, however, the company decided to pin its racing hopes on vee-twins, and the machine seen here is one of three built to contest the 1914 Senior TT, the team of riders comprising Harry and Charlie Collier, together with Bert Colver.

The 1914 TT model was very little changed from that of the previous year, and was powered by a 496 cc MAG (Motosacoche, Acacias, Geneva) overhead-valve engine with possibly the world's first hemispherical combustion chamber. Contemporary press reports indicated that the main improvements over the previous year's model included cast-iron pistons instead of steel, and Stauffer-type greasers to lubricate the valve gear rockers — cunningly placed so that when hot the grease would run down the rocker spindles. It was said also that 'the principal parts have been considerably strengthened wherever it has been considered advisable to do so'.

As originally built the three TT machines employed belt drive and incorporated a three-speed Armstrong Triplex gear in the rear hub (really just a king-size version of the hub gearing familiar to all touring pedal cyclists). But the countershaft gearbox was rapidly making headway, and its superiority over hub gears was very soon demonstrated.

Charlie Collier, for instance, didn't even complete the first lap of the 1914 Senior race,

he dropped out on the mountain when the hub gears stripped. Even Bert Colver, who was to be among the leaders from the start and who would run home in a fine fourth place, had his troubles and was forced to complete the last two laps stuck in the 4.5 to 1 middle ratio. As for Harry Collier, on the third works Matchless, he looked all set for a win and was holding a firm lead when, approaching Sulby Bridge, the frame suddenly broke at 70 mph. Harry was flung down the road and was lucky to escape with nothing more than bruises.

The experiences of that meeting must have convinced the Matchless management that it was time to discard hub gears, and we can assume that conversion of the machine we see here to a countershaft gearbox and all-chain drive was carried out as soon as possible thereafter. Certainly the complete team of the Collier brothers and Colver, with the 496 cc Matchless-MAG models, took part in the Motor Cycling Club's Sixth Annual Meeting at Brooklands on 18 July, with Charlie and Bert finishing first and second in the up-to-560 cc event, while in the 'Invitation Club Despatch Race' — whatever that may have been — the winners were the Woolwich & Plumstead MCC, whose team consisted of Harry, Charlie and Bert. It is believed that the machine exhibited is the ex-Bert Colver model.

Specification

Make Matchless. **Model** Works TT. **Engine** 496 cc (64 × 77 mm bore and stroke) MAG overhead-valve vee-twin. **Power output** Not quoted. **Tyres** 26 × 2½ × 2 in beaded-edge, front and rear. **Frame** Brazed-lug single loop. **Suspension** Girder front forks with enclosed single spring. Rigid rear. **Weight** Not quoted. **Wheelbase** 58.25 in. **Manufacturer** H. Collier & Sons (Matchless) Ltd, Plumstead Road, London SE18.

Above Certainly one of the trio of Matchless works machines for the 1914 Senior TT, the model seen here is thought to have been ridden by Bert Colver into fourth place. **Right** Though Matchless would not make their own engines for several years yet, the low-built frame and enclosed-spring girder front forks were their own manufacture. **Far right** Originally, transmission was by direct vee-belt to a three-speed rear hub. The countershaft gearbox and chain drive are later modifications. **Below** Power unit of the 1914 Matchless is a Swiss-built MAG ohv vee-twin. The makers still exist.

1951 497 cc Matchless G80C Trials

One of the major suppliers of motorcycles to the British Forces during World War 2, Matchless were the first to announce a civilian range following the cessation of hostilities. This they did in June 1945 — though, of course, the machines were essentially civilianized versions of those that had been produced for the military. They were first, also, to announce the production of post-war competitions models in March 1946.

There were no more than fifty in that initial batch, comprising twenty 497 cc Model G80C and thirty 347 cc G3LC, but at least it was a start. But note that these were 'competitions' mounts, for at that time motorcycle sport was far less specialized than it became later and the same model was considered suitable for either trials or scrambles, any modifications which the customer may have thought necessary being up to him.

The G80C and G3LC were substantially the same, apart from engine size, and featured a special steering head angle, altered fork trail, higher ground clearance, special exhaust system, folding kickstarter pedal, light-alloy mudguards and competition tyres. The frame, however, was still, in effect, the old military pattern.

Leading Matchless trials rider of the immediate post-war period was Yorkshire's Artie Ratcliffe (he was to win the Scottish Six-Days Trial in 1950 and 1954) but as time went on it seemed that Plumstead tended to rely more heavily on the associated AJS make for trials success, while looking to Matchless for victory in the scrambles field.

From 1949, hairpin valve springs were employed, but the next year brought a more notable change in that the competitions models were given light-alloy cylinders and head, Lucas 'wader' waterproofed magnetos and longer front fork springs.

By 1951, in which year our example was manufactured, the day of the all-round competitions model was passing and polarization into specific trials and scrambles mounts was taking over. However, the parting was not yet complete. AMC offered the big Matchless single in rigid-frame form (as still preferred by the serious trials rider) but now there was the option of swinging-arm rear suspension controlled by those fat little AMC-built damper units which motorcyclists termed 'jampots'. However, the brochure did say that the sprung models were essentially for such events such as the ISDT.

Production of competitions bikes was still on a limited scale, a small batch being produced each spring, and another small batch in the autumn. For the 1951 G80C Trials there was now a small 2¼-gallon steel fuel tank raised from the frame tank-mounting lugs on distance pieces, and the rubber saddle was mounted very high — which could have suited long-legged characters, but most have given shorties a deal of difficulty when a crafty dab was needed to maintain forward progress up a rocky gully.

If truth be told, though, the 'five-hundred' was a heavy and ungainly model, and the factory's own trials teamsters much preferred to use the 'three-fifty'. Not until 1953 (for the 1954 season) did the factory produce a lighter, all-welded trials frame in manganese-steel tubing (it afforded, also, an increase in ground clearance). Later in 1954 the entire AMC team switched to rear-sprung models, and the day of the rigid trials machine drew to a close.

Specification

Make Matchless. **Model** G80C Trials. **Engine** 497 cc (82.5 × 93 mm bore and stroke) overhead-valve single. **Power output** 23 bhp at 5,400 rpm. **Tyres** 3.00 × 21 in front, 4.00 × 19 in rear. **Frame** Brazed-lug tubular diamond. **Suspension** Oil-damped telescopic front forks. Rigid rear. **Weight** 307 lb dry. **Wheelbase** 53 in. **Manufacturer** Associated Motor Cycles Ltd, Plumstead Road, London SE18.

Above Rear springing on trials machines was not yet fully accepted by riders of 1951, but swinging-arm suspension was an option on the G80C. **Right** With very few modifications, the frame and Teledraulic front forks were still, in essence, those of the wartime despatch-rider G3L model. **Far right** A light-alloy cylinder barrel and head had been introduced the previous year, but cast-in pushrod tunnels were still a long way off. **Below** Tiny and high-mounted, the rubber saddle was not to every rider's taste. Rear damper units are AMC's own-make, nicknamed 'Jampots'.

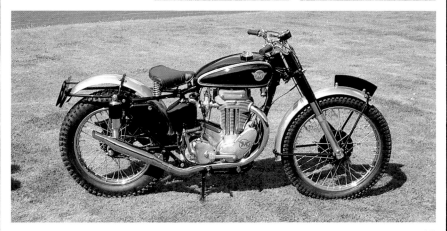

1955 498 cc Matchless G45

The thing about the G45 is that it was never really designed as a racing machine, but was derived from the road-going Matchless G9 Super Clubman vertical twin — the one which, unique among British vertical twins, employed a centre bearing which was claimed to overcome the inherent vibration of this type of engine. In the years immediately after World War 2 the AMC combine, makers of AJS and Matchless, had a successful 350 cc racer for the private entrant in the 350 cc Model 7R AJS, but there was no equivalent over-the-counter racing model in the 500 cc class.

The factory itself went racing, using the celebrated Porcupine twins (originally intended to be supercharged, although the post-war ban on blowers by the FIM meant that the Porcupine — so named from the spiky cylinder-head finning of the early version — never did have the chance to show its true potential) but this machine was too complex and too expensive to be considered for replica production.

So why not, one may well ask, overbore and stroke a Model 7R to produce a competitive 500 cc racing single? That is exactly what the Plumstead people did do... The outcome was the well-respected Matchless G50. Meanwhile ten of the Super Clubman twins had been prepared for the 1951 Senior Clubmans TT in the Isle of Man, some running as Matchlesses, the others under an AJS tank badge. To be honest they weren't all that competitive, but work on the models had given the factory's racing shop an idea, so for the 1951 Senior Manx Grand Prix a new machine embracing a rather modified G9 power unit installed in a 7R frame was built, to be raced by Robin Sherry.

Down below it looked a fairly standard G9, but the cylinder heads were something special, with finning carried well up the sides of the forward rocker-box; cylinders and heads were in light-alloy. The original intention had been to use the standard roadster nodular-iron crankshaft, but when the prototype was run up to full power on the test bed at Plumstead the shaft broke, and the driving half, plus the dynamometer coupling, went whizzing round the shop chipping lumps out of the concrete while the test staff cowered and waited for peace. So, hurriedly, an all-steel crankshaft was made and fitted, and the engine shipped to the Island with little time to spare. In the race Robin Sherry finished fourth, but he admitted that the vibration was awesome to experience.

Nevertheless it was a start, and the G45 was on its way, with Australian Ernie Ring giving it a reasonable outing in the 1952 Senior TT until a crash eliminated him. The same September Derek Farrant had a start-to-finish win in the Senior MGP — naughty, because works models weren't supposed to run in the Manx — and a month later production plans for the model, now officially called the G45, were announced. It would continue in production until 1957, after which the new G50 single took over, but though the twin was never a total success as a solo racer it did achieve fame as a sidecar outfit power plant, especially in the hands of Pip Harris or Colin Seeley. And it did make a wholly satisfying noise!

Our example comes from 1955, almost at the end of the model's development, and it incorporates the forged-steel crankshaft which that year supplanted the original machined-from-solid type.

Specification

Make Matchless. **Model** G45. **Engine** 498 cc (66 × 72 mm bore and stroke) overhead-valve vertical twin. **Power output** 48 bhp at 7,200 rpm. **Tyres** 3.00 × 19 in front, 3.50 × 19 in rear. **Frame** All-welded duplex tubular loops. **Suspension** Oil-damped telescopic front forks. Swinging-arm rear forks controlled by spring and hydraulic units. **Weight** 320 lb dry. **Wheelbase** 55.5 in. **Manufacturer** Associated Motor Cycles Ltd, Plumstead Road, London SE18.

Above With running gear derived from that of the successful Model 7R AJS, the Matchless G45 was the Plumstead factory's first essay into the 500 cc over-the-counter racing field. **Right** Never quite as effective as a solo racer as it should have been, the G45 twin nevertheless proved useful in sidecar racing. **Far right** Power unit was essentially a developed version of the roadster G9 twin; a forged crankshaft was new for 1955. **Below** In black, with silver lining, the Matchless was certainly easy on the eye — and the note of the twin cylinder engine pleased the ear, too!

1934 246 cc New Imperial Grand Prix 50

To workaday riders of the 1930s the New Imperial name was perhaps best known for the firm's sturdy little unit-construction 146 cc overhead-valve model, the Unit Minor with helical-gear primary drive. But the factory had, also, a long and very distinguished racing record both at home and overseas, to which riders of the calibre of Ken and Eddie Twemlow, Bert Le Vack, Ted Mellors, Charlie Dodson and Leo Davenport had contributed.

New Imperial had not just one but three bright pages in the history of racing. Les Archer, on a 246 cc model, was the first man to lap Brooklands at over 100 mph on a bike of that capacity. Ginger Wood, on the works 492 cc vee-twin (in effect, the upper works of two of the 'two-fifty' machines on a common crankcase) was first to pack 100 miles into an hour on British soil using a British-made multi-cylinder, thereby winning *The Motor Cycle*'s silver cup. And Bob Foster, in 1936, was the last man to win the 250 cc Lightweight TT on a wholly British-made machine.

The Model 50 as pictured here was manufactured in the 1934 and 1935 seasons only (there was also a 346 cc version) and was a series-production racer for the private runner, embodying the considerable experience of the firm's own racing team. In the 1933 season, to take just one year, 'New Imps' had taken the Lightweight TT makers' team prize, and had won the Dutch TT and the German, Belgian, Ulster and Swedish Grands Prix.

Introducing the new Model 50 Grand Prix, the 1934 New Imperial catalogue claimed: 'These Grand Prix models, being designed on exactly the same lines as our actual TT models, are capable of *very high speeds*. Their general layout makes them pre-eminent for the fast sporting rider.' It certainly looked the part, with the characteristic New Imperial pistol-grip fuel tank, footchange gearbox and TT carburettor. The price was 58 guineas, but for a further £5 7s it could be supplied in fast-roadster guise complete with full lighting equipment including a 'racing Lucas Magdyno'. Another optional fitting was a bronze cylinder head at £5 extra.

As supplied from the works, the machine had a compression ratio of 7.5 to 1, but under the cylinder base flange were two 1/32 in thick compression plates. Take out one plate and the compression ratio was raised to 7.75 to 1, take out both and it went up to 8 to 1.

The Motor Cycle road tested a 246 cc Model 50 in January 1934, at first with BTH racing magneto and without lighting, when a mean speed of 77 mph was reached. Later, full electrics and the 'racing Magdyno' were substituted and this time the mean speed reached was 70 mph. Interestingly, for a machine with such a sporting specification, the engine was very light on petrol, returning 81 mpg at an average of 35 mph.

Works entries for the 1934 Lightweight TT looked much like the production models, except that the engines made much use of magnesium alloy castings and the cylinder barrel was in light-alloy. Of course the production race models weren't quite so exotic, but the catalogued Model 50 for 1935 did at least offer an all-alloy engine at extra cost.

Specification

Make New Imperial. **Model** Grand Prix 50. **Engine** 246 cc (62.5 × 80 mm bore and stroke) overhead-valve single. **Power output** Not quoted. **Tyres** 3.00 × 21 in front and rear. **Frame** Brazed-lug duplex tubular loop. **Suspension** Girder front forks with friction damping. Rigid rear. **Weight** 299 lb dry. **Wheelbase** 54 in. **Manufacturer** New Imperial Motors Ltd, Spring Road, Hall Green, Birmingham 28.

Above The New Imperial failed to return to the market after World War 2, but in pre-war days its racing reputation was formidable. The 246 cc Grand Prix was a highly successful production model. **Right** Sporty looks do not bely the New Imp's character. **Far right** Engine design was New Imperial's own. A bronze head is evident here, but in the following season an all-alloy engine was offered at extra cost. **Below** The 'pistol grip' tank shape was seen also on the firm's 500 cc racing twin. On test, the Grand Prix reached 77 mph — very good going for a 1934 'two-fifty'.

1907 944 cc NLG-Peugeot Racing Special

Never heard of an NLG? That isn't surprising, for the initials are those of North London Garages, a company active in motorcycle manufacture in a small way between the years of 1905 and 1912 only. Nevertheless the NLG certainly left an indelible mark on the pages of motorcycle racing history, when Will (known as 'Wee-Wee') Cook raced away from the field to win — by over half a mile — the first-ever official motorcycle event to be organized on Brooklands track near Weybridge, Surrey.

The track had in fact been finished a year earlier (and there had been an unofficial motorcycle match race won by Gordon McMinnies) but not until Easter Monday, 20 April 1908 were motorcycles brought into the programme with ACU blessing. The event was a two-lap (5½ mile) scratch race for machines not exceeding 80 × 98 mm per cylinder, and it attracted 21 entries including the already-famous Charlie and Harry Collier, mounted respectively on their International Cup and 1907 TT Matchless racers.

Originally, Cook's NLG, which was and still is powered by an automatic-inlet-valve French-built Peugeot vee-twin engine, was right on the limit at 80 × 98 mm, but in preparation for the race the engine was stroked, so that it came to the line at 944 cc (80 × 94 mm). During practice on the preceding Tuesday he had been reported as covering more than 30 miles at an average of over 68 mph. However, race day proved to be windy, and on his 2.625 to 1 top — indeed only — gear, Cook was over-geared and the bike was running at 5 mph below its practice form.

Nevertheless, the ultra-light NLG — perforated wherever possible without losing essential strength — had more than enough in hand to dispose of the opposition, and Cook happily collected the 20-guinea prize purse — a small fortune by 1908 standards.

Cook and his formidable NLG again made Brooklands history a year later when, in June 1909, the BMCRC staged a members-only race meeting. Cook won the all-comers scratch race, but that was just a warm-up, and the big sensation came later in the afternoon when a truck transported competitors to the Railway Straight, there to take part in a series of timed runs over measured half-mile, kilometre, and mile distances, with a flying start in each case. Returning speeds of 75.898, 75.921 and 75.678 mph respectively in each section, the NLG put up the Fastest Time of Day by a tremendous margin.

However, the machine's spell in the limelight was coming to an end and in 1910 both it and its rider retired from the scene, Will Cook to devote his time to building-up the Weymouth garage business he had established with his brother. He died in 1949 and it was discovered that the famous old racing machine still existed, stored in the premises of W. E. & F. L. Cook at Weymouth. Ownership of the model passed to his son, P. W. Cook, and a reminiscent article appeared in a 1951 issue of *Motor Cycling*. Eventually, in 1960, Mr Cook agreed to let the late John Griffith restore his father's old bike for future exhibition. 'Originally', revealed John, 'the cylinders were copper plated. Restoration would have meant replating the bores, and since it was not intended that the engine would run again, the cylinders were given an external copper-spray finish'.

It was eventually acquired for the National Motorcycle Museum collection and, after further external restoration, took its rightful place in the competitions' Hall of Fame.

Specification

Make NLG. **Model** Racing Special. **Engine** Peugeot 944 cc (80 × 94 mm bore and stroke) automatic inlet valve, side exhaust vee-twin, with coil ignition and hand-operated oil pump. **Power output** Not quoted. **Tyres** 26 × 2 in front and rear, wired-edge. **Frame** Brazed-lug tubular lightweight. **Suspension** None; rigid front forks with added bracing. **Weight** 200 lb. **Wheelbase** 48 in. **Manufacturer** North London Garages, Corsica Street, Highbury, London.

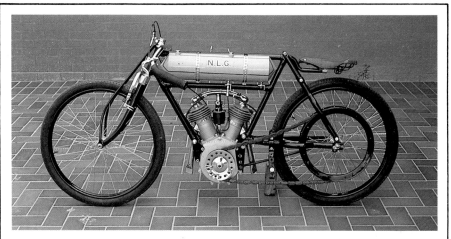

Above Ridden by Will Cook, this spartan machine was the winner in 1908 of the first-ever motor cycle race at Brooklands. No springing of any kind is provided. **Right** Brooklands was notoriously bumpy, and the front forks had additional bracing as a precaution against breakage. **Far right** Cast on the crankcase, the 'PF' initials identify the famous French firm of Peugeot Freres. Throttle and ignition levers are mounted on the tank side. **Below** The saddle position of the NLG looks most precarious. Now copper-sprayed for preservation, the cylinders were originally copper plated.

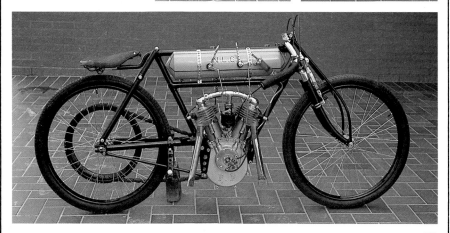

1920-21 490 cc Norton Racing

Though outright success in the Isle of Man may have eluded them (except, of course, for Rem Fowler's 1907 twin-cylinder-class win on a Peugeot-engined model), nevertheless Norton were already well established in the racing world by the time of the 1914–18 war, and they quickly returned to that field after the end of the war.

When racing was resumed the factory relied for the first three years on the 490 cc (79 × 100 mm bore and stroke) side-valve engine, designed by James Lansdowne Norton himself, which was in fact the forerunner of the famous 16H so familiar to despatch riders of the 1939–45 conflict.

The close of World War 1 had seen Norton Motors move from the original cramped premises in Floodgate Street, Birmingham, to the address that was to become world famous — Bracebridge Street, Aston. For the production race models (the Brooklands Special and Brooklands Road Special), the firm continued to specify belt drive and single gearing, but for the 1920 TT races — the first to be held following the wartime break — a three-speed gearbox and all-chain drive was adopted. Internally, the engine abandoned a plain big-end bearing in favour of rollers running direct on the crankpin, and a tapered H-section connecting rod with an oilway drilled from big-end to little-end.

In most other respects the works model was the standard sports model, though with footrests instead of footboards, a new toolbox (!), no kick-starter and two rear brakes to supplement the bicycle-type stirrup front brake.

Norton were pinning their Senior TT hopes on Graham Walker, Douggie Brown and Vic Horsman, and though Walker suffered facial injuries when he ran into a stray sheep on the mountain section of the course during early-morning practice, he recovered in time to take his place on the starting grid. There were fourteen Nortons in the entry, though not all were being looked after by team manager D. R. O'Donovan, and many of the private entries were of the older belt-drive type. The works models now featured a new three-speed Sturmey-Archer gearbox affording 4, 5 and 7.5 to 1 overall ratios, and a non-positive-stop gear pedal. Estimated speed in top gear was 76 mph, with 55 mph available in second.

Unhappily, from the Norton point of view, they missed Senior TT victory by only ten seconds after Douggie Brown, a Manxman who had ridden in every TT meeting from 1910, had tussled mightily with the strong Sunbeam contingent of George Dance, Tommy de la Hay and Eric Williams. As the last lap had begun, Brown trailed de la Hay by only seven seconds, but it seemed the Sunbeam man had something in reserve for his final lap was his fastest and Brown could find no reply.

However, the race did highlight Norton's record of reliability, for eight of the fifteen finishers were on the Bracebridge Street product. After the event, Brown revealed that on the fourth lap, when he was leading, he was given pit signals to ease off, otherwise he was sure he could have won. Interestingly, in the Douglas Promenade Sprint, held on the morning after the Senior TT, Brown and de la Hay dead-heated in 33.8 seconds for the flying kilometre, in the special class for actual TT starters and their machines.

Changes for the 1921 season were very few, though some of the works models were equipped with Webb internal-expanding front brake drums; but the day of the racing side-valve was nearly over anyway.

Specification

Make Norton. **Model** Racing. **Engine** 490 cc (79 × 100 mm bore and stroke) side-valve single. **Power output** 12 bhp at 4,300 rpm. **Tyres** 650 × 65 mm beaded-edge, front and rear. **Frame** Brazed-lug tubular diamond. **Suspension** Druid side-spring tubular girder front forks. Rigid rear. **Weight** 252 lb dry. **Wheelbase** 56.5 in. **Manufacturer** Norton Motors Ltd, Bracebridge Street, Aston, Birmingham 6.

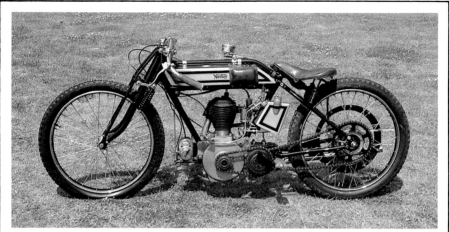

Above For the 1920 and 1921 seasons, Nortons still pinned their racing hopes on the J.L. Norton-designed 490 cc side-valve, though belt-drive was at last giving way to all-chain transmission. **Right** Dropped handlebars were accepted practice on racing models, allowing the rider to adopt a wind-cheating stance. **Far right** Exceptionally long-lived, the 490 cc (79 × 100 mm) side-valve was still powering British Army 16H machines in World War 2. **Below** Not an ounce is wasted, the racing Norton weighing only 252 lb in track trim.

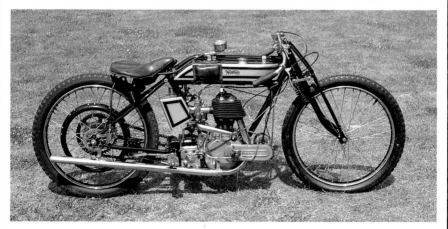

1928 490 cc Norton CS1

The mid-1920s certainly seemed to be the age of the overhead-camshaft engine as, inspired by the success of Velocette's 350 cc Model K (the prototype of which appeared in 1924), one factory after another followed fashion by developing a 'cammy' of their own. Norton had been late in producing even a pushrod overhead-valve engine, in 1922, but in the next couple of years development proceeded apace. By 1926, though, the firm felt that they had gone almost as far as they could with this type of power unit (bearing in mind the technology of the day) and so Walter Moore, who had joined Norton from the Douglas factory in 1924, laid out an entirely new ohc engine.

Strangely, this engine was not Norton property. Moore had designed the unit in his own time and when he left the firm, some years later, to join NSU in Germany he took the design with him. The outcome was a very Norton-looking NSU (it was said, wittily, that the NSU initials now meant 'Norton Spares Used'). But a further outcome was that Arthur Carroll was given the job of designing another ohc engine, the one which would be known as the famous Manx.

Walter Moore's engine was characterized by the shaft-and-bevel method of taking the drive to the overhead camshaft (the camshaft itself ran in a separate cambox carried on the cylinder head), the bottom set of bevel gears being housed in a long 'blister' on the right-hand crankcase half, its length being due to the fact that beneath the bevel gears was a reciprocating oil pump.

To house the new engine there was a frame in which the front down and seat tubes ran into a cradle under the engine and Sturmey-Archer gearbox. Webb girder forks were fitted, as also were substantial internal-expanding brakes at front and rear. It was not a foot-change gearbox in the true sense of the word, but the gear lever was mounted horizontally and — in the same manner as adopted by wartime despatch riders using the Model H Triumph — it afforded secure top

and bottom ratios, but second was hit-or-miss.

For the TT, the Norton team adopted a belt-and-braces outlook, and they took to the Isle of Man not only a trio of new ohc models but also some of the older pushrod machines. In fact it was Joe Craig in person who was first to venture out in practice on the 'cammy', the rest of the team following suit later. In the actual 1927 Senior TT Stanley Woods looked to have it in the bag, and led for the first four laps until a burnt-out clutch sent him to the dead-machine park. Craig was nowhere in the running as he had lost valuable minutes at the start with a crankcase full of oil. But Alec Bennett retrieved Bracebridge Street honour with a fine win, reporting afterwards that the new ohc Norton steered 'wonderfully well'.

It was no surprise, therefore, when Norton added a production version of the machine to their programme for 1928. Star of the Olympia Show, it was given the designation CS1 (or Camshaft Model No 1). Announcing the machine, *The Motor Cycle* commented that: 'Except for minor modifications the overhead-camshaft Norton, perhaps the most attractive machine in the range, will remain substantially the same as when it made its first appearance in the TT races'. You couldn't say fairer than that.

Specification

Make Norton. **Model** CS1. **Engine** 490 cc (79 × 100 mm bore and stroke) single overhead camshaft single. **Power output** Not quoted. **Tyres** 3.25 × 19 in front and rear. **Frame** Brazed-lug tubular cradle. **Suspension** Webb tubular girder front forks. Rigid rear. **Weight** 330 lb dry. **Wheelbase** 55 in. **Manufacturer** Norton Motors Ltd, Bracebridge Street, Aston, Birmingham 6.

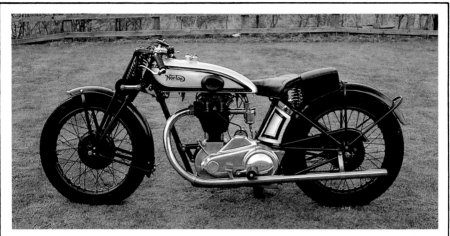

Above In Norton parlance, 'CS1' meant 'Camshaft Model No 1', a design from the drawing board of Walter Moore, housed in a new-style cradle frame. Boosted by Alec Bennett's 1927 TT win, the CS1 entered production for the 1928 season. **Right** Inverted-type handlebar levers were still the fashion; magneto drive was on the nearside. **Far right** Immediately recognizable is the CS1's long 'blister' on the crankcase, housing the lower bevels and the oil pump. **Below** The old adage of 'If it looks right, it is right' certainly applied to the cammy Norton!

1952 490 cc Norton 500T Trials Combination

Bracebridge Street's association with motorcycle trials went back a very long way indeed, and even in the 1920s they were offering, for trials use, machines constructed to 'Colonial Specification' with higher ground clearance and high-level exhaust. By 1937, the Norton catalogue illustrated a machine that looked both pretty and purposeful; however, it was not yet a trials model in its own right and, instead, it represented a specification to which any bike in the programme could be built to order.

Again there were the high-ground-clearance frame and upswept exhaust, but now there was also a wide-ratio gearbox, folding kick-starter, quick-action twistgrip and chromium-plated mudguards, primary chaincase and rear chainguard, and brake plates.

A particular reason for the firm's interest in trials, of course, was that British Sidecar Trials Champion, Dennis Mansell, was the son of Norton's long-serving managing director. Dennis would himself be appointed a director in 1938, and when he retired from active sport the national D. K. Mansell Sidecar Trial was instituted in his honour.

In the immediate post-war Norton programme, the policy of offering a trials specification for the standard roadsters was continued, but meanwhile a proper trials model as such was under development. Mention of this was first made in the press in November of 1948 where it was termed the 'Ohv Comp 500'. Later that month it made its Earls Court Show debut as the 500T, and though a smaller 350T version was promised for later production, only a small number appear to have been made.

The 500T, however, turned out to be one of the most handsome trials machines ever built and it achieved almost immediate popularity. Sales were boosted by the success of the factory's own trials team, which included John Draper, Rex Young and Geoff Duke, for although Geoff was to become one of the all-time greats of road racing in fact it was as a trials exponent that he first came to the attention of factory bosses.

The engine of the new model was derived from that of the ES2 roadster, but was given a light-alloy cylinder barrel and head. For trials work, low-speed torque rather than high revs is the requirement, and so compression ratio was no more than 6 to 1. The gearbox was that of the International models, but with wide ratios affording overall gearing of 5.5, 8.1, 13.15 and 18 to 1. No lighting was provided, and the magneto was a BTH waterproof type.

Essentially the frame was that of the wartime 16H, but considerably lightened and heightened. Carried on three rubber mountings was a shapely 2½-gallon fuel tank finished in dull chrome plating and set far enough back from the steering head to permit 100 degrees of steering lock. Wheel rims were in high-tensile steel, so allying strength and lightness. The small Dunlop rubber saddle could be adjusted for height to suit the rider's taste.

Popular not only among solo men, the 500T made its mark in sidecar trials also, and it is shown here attached to a typical trials sidecar of the early to mid-1950s, with sheet-alloy bodywork. Comfort for the passenger was a minor consideration, and a trials chair was judged on the ease with which the crewman could move his body weight around when required, to keep the outfit on an even keel around tricky turns and on adverse cambers.

Specification

Make Norton. **Model** 500T Trials Combination. **Engine** 490 cc (79 × 100 mm bore and stroke) overhead-valve single. **Power output** 21 bhp at 5,000 rpm. **Tyres** 2.75 × 21 in front, 4.00 × 19 in rear. **Frame** Brazed-lug tubular diamond. **Suspension** Oil-damped telescopic front forks. Rigid rear. **Weight** 300 lb dry. **Wheelbase** 53 in. **Manufacturer** Norton Motors Ltd, Bracebridge Street, Aston, Birmingham 6.

Above Trials sidecar outfits have changed considerably since the days of the 500T Norton; today's chairs are even more spartan, and built in glass-fibre. **Right** Close co-operation is needed between driver and crewman. The sidecar handrail is necessary for passenger acrobatics. **Far right** Though based on the road-going Model ES2, the 500T power unit has the benefit of light-alloy cylinder and head. **Below** Much coveted by Pre-65 Trial exponents of today, the Norton 500T was one of the most handsome trials machines ever built. Wheel rims were made in high-tensile steel, to provide lightness and strength.

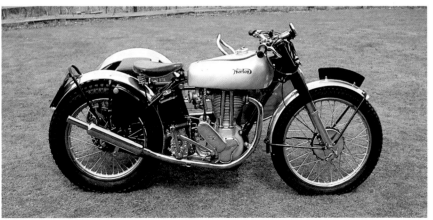

1954 349 cc Norton Outside-flywheel Experimental

To the race enthusiast manning the roadsides at the May 1954 international road race meeting at Floreffe (Belgium) there seemed nothing unusual about the pair of Manx models ridden into second place in both the 350cc and 500 cc races by Norton's race team leader, Rhodesian Ray Amm. But a closer glance in the paddock would have revealed a large-diameter outside flywheel, carried inboard of the engine sprocket on each machine.

In fact Ray was giving a pre-season tryout to the latest products of the Bracebridge Street race shop, on which Joe Craig and his team had been working all winter. The trouble was that the Manx was no longer the invincible machine it used to be and, faced with increasing competition from the Italian four-cylinder models, Norton had opted to stay with the single but to wring still-higher rpm from the ageing design.

To cut down on piston speed, bores had been increased and strokes shortened, so that the 349 cc was now 78 × 73 mm bore and stroke, while the 499 cc version was now a '90-bore', with dimensions of 90 × 78.4 mm. The reduced stroke meant that shorter and stiffer connecting rods could now be employed. Moreover, crankcase dimensions were much reduced because the inside flywheels (a source of oil-drag) had been elminated and, instead, there was the aforementioned outside flywheel. To carry the extra drive-side load, the former single-row roller and ball bearings in that location were superseded by a heavy-duty, double-row caged roller.

'The larger the diameter of a flywheel', explained *The Motor Cycle*, describing the new models, 'the lighter it can be for a given flywheel effect … and flywheel diameter is no longer limited by the need to keep the overall engine height, and hence the crankcase size, down sufficiently for easy installation in the frame'.

Other engine changes included new cam profiles and larger valves to give more efficient breathing. The increase in engine rpm was reflected in the adoption of a shortened exhaust system. To improve chain life there was a rubber-element engine shaft shock absorber and the gearbox was, for the first time, a five-speeder of Burman make, with five-plate clutch. Reducing frame tube thickness of the 350 cc model from 16 gauge to 17 gauge saved some weight, but the frame was in any case smaller than before.

On his first Isle of Man practice appearance with the 348 cc outside-flywheel machine Ray Amm lapped at a useful 94.40 mph, but success was to elude him in the actual race (when the bike was fitted with the famous long-nose fairing) and he dropped out at Kirkmichael with engine trouble while leading. Consolation came when Ray, on the 500 cc version, was declared winner of the storm-lashed and shortened Senior race.

For the 1955 season the outside flywheel, small crankcase idea was to have been taken further with the new F-type horizontal engine which, on test, was producing more power at the rear wheel than the 1954 model did at the crankshaft. But Norton management decided they could no longer afford special racing models and henceforth (for a year or two, anyway) the team would be mounted on standard Manx machines.

The 1954 Ray Amm 'three-fifty' seen here therefore represents the last of the Joe Craig specials ever to take to the track, and marks the end of an era.

Specification

Make Norton. **Model** Experimental. **Engine** 349 cc (78 × 73 mm bore and stroke) double overhead-camshaft single. **Power output** Not quoted. **Tyres** 3.00 × 19 in front, 3.50 × 19 in rear. **Frame** All-welded parallel twin tubular loops. **Suspension** Oil-damped telescopic front forks. Swinging-arm rear forks controlled by spring and hydraulic units. **Weight** 309 lb dry. **Wheelbase** 54.5 in. **Manufacturer** Norton Motors Ltd, Bracebridge Street, Aston, Birmingham 6.

Above First seen at Floreffe (Belgium) in the hands of Ray Amm, this experimental Norton employed a large outside flywheel between the crankcase and driving sprocket, so allowing smaller crankcase dimensions. **Right** To the crowds at the trackside, the Ray Amm Norton appeared to be the usual Featherbed-frame Manx. It was used for one season only. **Far right** Though few changes are noticeable in a timing-side view, in fact the engine was less tall, and the frame was a little lower. **Below** Internal engine changes meant that a much shortened exhaust system could be fitted.

1962 499 cc Norton 30M Manx

Was there ever a series-production racing motorcycle so long-lived, so respected, or so consistently successful as the Manx Norton? Its ancestry could be traced back to the early 1930s, when Arthur Carroll was charged with the work of laying out anew the overhead-camshaft engine originally designed in 1920s by Walter Moore. Initially it was not termed 'Manx' — at least not officially — but was a version of the super-sporting but roadgoing International built, to customer's order, to racing specification. The 'Manx' tag was adopted by Norton Motors post-war, batches of the models being built, season by season, until the final batch of all left the factory at Bracebridge Street, Aston, in 1962.

The machine in the National Motorcycle Museum's collection is one of that last batch, and so we see the Manx Norton representing its last flowering. Yet maybe the wonder is that the design lasted for so long, for in the late 1930s, as war clouds loomed on the horizon, it seemed that the unsupercharged racing single had reached and passed its prime, soon to be relegated to the ranks of the also-rans by blown multi-cylinder machines from Italy and German.

What gave it a further and rather unexpected lease of life was the banning, when international racing was resumed in post-war days, of supercharged engines. The Norton company produced the Manx for sale to the enthusiastic privateers who formed the bulk of the entry in races both at home and abroad but, also, the factory maintained its own racing team. It had, too, a tame wizard by the name of Joe Craig who managed, unfailingly, to wring yet another horsepower or two from the long-in-the-tooth engine ready for the start of each season, to keep the Norton name well to the forefront.

And Norton kept faith with their customers, passing on the secrets of the works motors a season or so later, to be incorporated in the production models. So the original single overhead-camshaft models made way for double-knockers, the long-stroke configu-ration was superseded by shorter-stroke engines aimed at reducing piston speed (and hence wear), and so on.

But as the 1950s rolled on, even Joe Craig had to admit that the Manx was reaching the end of the line, and that each minor increase in power was achieved at the expense of reliability. There was to have been a new racing Norton, with horizontal engine (it was built but never tried in anger), followed by a racing four on which preliminary work was begun... But it never came to pass. Norton's parent group, AMC, was running short of money, works support of racing ceased in 1955 (in which year Joe Craig retired) and little further development of the Manx took place. Soon after this particular machine was built, in 1962, even the hallowed factory at Bracebridge Street was closed, with production of Norton roadsters, but not racers, being transferred to the parent factory at Plumstead.

A last word or so. The machine seen here is a 'Featherbed' Manx. Why so? Because when the famous double-loop frame was first used in 1950, works rider Harold Daniell said that riding the new machine was, by comparison with the old plunger-sprung 'Garden Gate' Manx, like 'lying on a feather bed'. The name stuck, and in due course the Norton catalogue would include roadsters singles and twins, equally featherbedded. There was indeed truth in the old saying that 'racing improves the breed'.

Specification

Make Norton. **Model** 30M Manx. **Engine** 499 cc (86 × 85.8 mm bore and stroke) double overhead-camshaft single. **Power output** 47 bhp at 6,500 rpm. **Tyres** 3.00 × 19 in front, 3.50 × 19 in rear. **Frame** All-welded, parallel twin tubular loops. **Suspension** Oil-damped telescopic front forks. Swinging arm rear forks controlled by spring and hydraulic units. **Weight** 313 lb dry. **Wheelbase** 54.5 in. **Manufacturer** Norton Motors Ltd, Bracebridge Street, Aston, Birmingham 6.

Above In 1962 the legendary Manx Norton reached the end of the line. This is one of the final 499 cc double-ohc 30M models in all its classic simplicity. **Below** Megaphone exhaust (flattened, for clearance when cornering) identifies the 499 cc Manx, the equivalent 348 cc model having a smaller, reverse-cone megaphone. **Right** Slim build of the single-cylinder Norton aids penetration, but riders usually fitted a dolphin fairing anyway. **Far right** Over the years, camshaft-drive mechanism was improved and finning area increased, but exposed hairpin valve springs remained to the bitter end. Riders padded the spring area with sponge rubber to absorb oil fling.

1950 346 cc Royal Enfield Works Trials

Although the Redditch (Worcestershire) based Royal Enfield company didn't interest themselves overmuch in either road-racing or scrambles, their impact on the world of trials was very great indeed. In 1946 alone, Royal Enfield riders won two premier awards, 26 cups, and seventeen lesser tropies in major British trials (or so their sales literature claimed) but the firm's major contribution to the story of trials came in 1947, with the introduction of a competitions version of the rear-sprung 346 cc Bullet.

This machine ran contrary to the then-current precept that for success in trials one had to have a rigid rear frame, so that the wheel could find maximum grip. The Enfield had a true swinging-arm suspension system with spring-and-hydraulic units of the company's own design and manufacture (as they had to be, for proprietary firms such as Girling or Armstrong had not yet entered the market).

It was on 18 March 1949, that the Worcestershire licence office issued the factory with registration number HNP 331, which in the course of the years would become one of the two best-remembered numbers of all time (the other being Sammy Miller's Ariel, GOV 132). The first custodian of HNP 331 was Stan Holmes, but meanwhile a young lad named Johnny Brittain — son of pre- and immediate post-war ISDT teamster Vic Brittain — had been performing wonders in trials on a little 125 cc James two-stroke. Johnny was invited to join the Royal Enfield trials team in 1950 and was allocated HNP 331. That same autumn he rode it in the British Experts Trial.

With fuel rationing at last at an end, Brittain began to write a whole new chapter in the trials record book by winning, among other events, the national Allan Jefferies, Clayton and Travers Trials in 1951. That was just the start, and in the decade ahead he would win over fifty major trials, collect thirteen ISDT medals, achieve the coveted ACU Trials Star and win the Scottish Six-Days, Scott, and

British Experts Trials twice each. It got to the stage where one could scarcely open the pages of the weekly motorcycle press, without seeing a picture of 'Johnny Britt' and his legendary HNP 331 pobbling carefully up some incredibly rocky gulley.

However, it has to be confessed that it wasn't always the same HNP 331, for the number plates were transferred from one model to another as development progressed; usually they graced a 346 cc model, though they had been known to appear on a unit-construciton 248 cc Trials Crusader! So the challenge 'Will the real HNP 331 please stand up?' cannot truly be answered.

The machine as seen here represents the 1950 stage of its development, equipped with the new roadster-type frame (which superseded the earlier and heavier pattern) and Royal Enfield's own design of telescopic front forks (there were occasions when HNP 331 wore hybrid Royal Enfield-cum-BSA legs). It has single-sided light-alloy wheel hubs, and a light-alloy cylinder and head on magnesium-alloy crankcase castings. The crankcases had been widened, to allow room for a more substantial big-end bearing and timing-side main bearing, and the holding-down studs had been respaced to provide meatier cylinder head and base joint areas.

The revamped all-alloy engine (though not the mag-alloy crankcases) was transferred to production for the 1952 season onward. Racing, it used to be said, improves the breed; but as Royal Enfield demonstrated, so does trials participation.

Specification

Make Royal Enfield. **Model** Works Trials. **Engine** 346 cc (70 × 90 mm bore and stroke) overhead-valve single. **Power output** 17 bhp at 5,500 rpm. **Tyres** 3.00 × 21 in front, 4.00 × 19 in rear. **Frame** All-welded tubular diamond. **Suspension** Oil-damped telescopic front forks. Swinging-arm rear forks controlled by spring and hydraulic units. **Weight** 310 lb. **Wheelbase** 54 in. **Manufacturer** Enfield Cycle Co Ltd, Redditch, Worcestershire.

Above One of the most familiar of all trials machines, the Royal Enfield, carried Johnny Brittain to countless victories, and proved that rear-sprung machinery could indeed conquer the rough. **Right** HNP331 was one of the two best-known trials registration numbers in the country; hydraulically-damped front forks are Royal Enfield's own design. **Far right** The characteristic timing chest, with integral double-ended reciprocating oil pump, dated right back to the early 1930s. **Below** Supremely functional, the design allied a magnesium-alloy crankcase to a particularly well finned longstroke cylinder barrel.

1920 499 cc Rudge Multi TT Replica

In present-day parlance a 'multi' is a motorcycle with a multiplicity of cylinders, but in veteran and early-vintage days the term meant something very different — a Rudge with a patented expanding-pulley belt drive system which offered (within rather narrow limits) a range of gear ratios. As the sides of a vee-belt pulley are brought closer together, so the belt rides higher up the pulley and its effective diameter is thereby increased; draw the pulley flanges apart, the effective diameter is reduced, and so the ratio is lowered. So far so good, but the Rudge system went one better in that the engine shaft and rear wheel belt pulleys were linked by a mechanism, by which as one pulley was expanded the other contracted, so maintaining the driving belt in constant tension.

In its day, the Rudge Multi variable-speed system was highly successful, and it became a standard fitting on the company's production racer, named the TT Model. This machine was first listed in 1911, priced at £48 15s in racing trim, and in effect was the first true TT Replica available to the serious racing man.

Rudge themselves had their first Isle of Man win in the 1914 Senior TT, when Cyril Pullin — later to be better known as a designer — took the honours on a Rudge built to his own requirements. The engine was the familiar inlet-over-exhaust 499 cc single, but it was installed in a new frame with a sloping top tube which afforded a lower riding position and lower centre of gravity than on previous models.

The outbreak of World War 1 robbed the Rudge factory of the chance to exploit the TT success and so gain an increase in sales; a TT model with a frame similar to the Cyril Pullin machine was catalogued for 1915, but from the spring of 1916 no Rudge motorcycles, not even for military purposes, were produced and it was not until 1919 that the factory was able to get back to something approaching normal. Some development

work had continued during the war, however, and at the Olympia Motor Cycle Show in November 1919, a TT Model was again among the company's exhibits.

Press reports described this as being 'almost identical in every respect to the one used by Mr Cyril Pullin when he put up such a magnificent performance in winning the 1914 Tourist Trophy Race. This machine differs from the roadster, inasmuch as the frame slopes from the steering head to the saddle, giving a delightfully low riding position.'

Sales resulting from the Show were reasonable, but it soon became apparent that belt drive, no matter how clever its application, had had its day. Development of chain drive and the countershaft gearbox had been proceeding apace and the Rudge was becoming outclassed in racing. From July 1920, the new lower frame with sloping top tube was adopted for all Rudge models (and incidentally, production the previous month had reached thirty per day, the highest figure ever achieved by the factory).

The final official appearance of the Rudge Multi was in the 1922 Senior TT where, of the ten Rudges entered, five used the Multi system and the remaining five chain-drive and a three-speed gearbox. Sadly, there were nine retirements, and the only finisher of the ten was one of the gearbox versions, in fourteenth place.

Specification

Make Rudge. **Model** TT Multi Replica. **Engine** 499 cc (85 × 88 mm bore and stroke) inlet-over-exhaust single. **Power output** Not quoted. **Tyres** 2.25 × 26 in beaded edge, front and rear. **Frame** Brazed-lug tubular diamond. **Suspension** Tubular girder front forks. Rigid rear. **Weight** 188 lb. **Wheelbase** 56 in. **Manufacturer** Rudge-Whitworth Ltd, Crow Lane, Coventry, Warwickshire.

Above Based on the 1914 Senior TT winner, the post-war TT Replica entered production in 1920, but the day of the belt-drive model was already passing. **Right** A sloping frame top tube (for lower seat height) distinguished the post-First World War Rudge Multi. Also, fuel tank colour changed from silver to dark green. **Far right** Overhead inlet valve, side exhaust valve — the traditional Rudge arrangement. Senspray carburettor was made by an associated firm. **Below** The miniature mudguard pad was not intended for pillion carrying, but to help the rider crouch low when road racing.

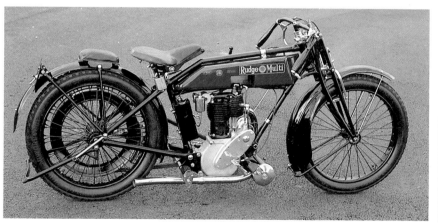

1933 499 cc Rudge TT Replica

Presided over by John Vernon Pugh, the well-known Coventry firm of Rudge-Whitworth was not exactly a stranger to road-racing victory — but in the late 1920s and early 1930s Rudge seemed to hit the racing jackpot; and not only road-racing, for the speedway Rudge was showing a clean pair of heels to the once all-conquering dirt Douglas.

Graham Walker's 1928 Ulster Grand Prix win inspired the never-to-be-forgotten 499 cc Rudge Ulster which topped the factory's road-going range, but in 1930 the racing squad of Walker, Tyrell Smith, Ernie Nott and Wal Handley virtually swept the board in the Isle of Man TT races, with first, second and third in the Junior race, first, second, sixth and seventh in the Senior, and the Manufacturers' Team Award in both.

Not unnaturally, it was decided to capitalize on this success by manufacturing TT Replica models, and the first entered the programme for the 1931 season. That year, the factory's own race models adopted a semi-radial four-valve cylinder head in which the inlet valves were parallel, but the exhaust valves were disposed radially and operated by a system of rocking levers.

However, that system would not be adopted on production TT Replica machines (which were at first listed in both 349 and 499 cc capacities) until 1933, the final year of their production. The first production TT Reps were full-radials — *exact* replicas of the successful 1930 TT Machines, as the brochure was careful to point out.

One might reasonably have expected that Rudge's outstanding road racing successes would have brought soaring sales of the road-going models, but there was another factor for which the firm had not bargained — the world recession which was the aftermath of the infamous Wall Street Crash. The TT Replica models sold well enough, and in the hands of local riders they began to gather awards far and wide.

At home, though, Rudge-Whitworth were running into financial trouble, and in an attempt to keep afloat they offered Rudge engines (under a Python name) to other manufacturers both at home and abroad. For some unexplained reason, the 350 and 500 TT Replicas for 1932 featured a forward-mounted magneto, but the 250 TT Replica, new for that season, carried the magneto at the rear of the cylinder.

Sadly, the sales figures continued to decline (they were running at only about 2,000 per year), and Rudge were forced to draw in their horns. An announcement issued in January 1933 gave the news that the firm was no longer able to support an official road racing team (though in fact Graham Walker formed the privateer Rudge Racing Syndicate, to which the firm lent the works racing models). But at least there would be production TT Replicas for 1933, and here we see that 499 cc model, now with semi-radial head. Note also the coupled front and rear brakes (for long a Rudge feature) and the steering damper which could be adjusted by means of a Bowden cable from a handlebar-mounted lever.

On 27 March 1933 a receiver and manager was appointed — though in fact production did continue, under a reconstitued company, and with a drastically chopped range of only four machines, the TT Replicas being among the casualties. Even that failed to stem the tide, and by mid-1935 Rudge were bankrupt, a situation from which they were rescued, somewhat unexpectedly, by EMI, the radio and records giant.

Specification

Make Rudge. **Model** TT Replica. **Engine** 499 cc (85 × 88 mm bore and stroke) four-valve overhead-valve single. **Power output** Not quoted. **Tyres** 3.00 × 21 in front, 3.25 × 20 in rear. **Frame** Brazed-lug tubular diamond. **Suspension** Tubular girder front forks with enclosed spring. Rigid rear. **Weight** 290 lb dry. **Wheelbase** 55.5 in. **Manufacturer** Rudge-Whitworth Ltd, Crow Lane, Coventry, Warwickshire.

Above This was the final year of the Rudge TT Replica, and for the first and only time the works-type semi-radial cylinder was adopted. **Right** Braking was a Rudge strong point, and the Replica featured the renowned coupled-braking system with proportional loading. **Far right** Not until the later 1930s would Rudge employ totally-enclosed valve gear, and in 1933 everything was still out in the open. **Below** Finance difficulties meant that Rudge were unable to take full advantage of their race successes, but club riders, with their businesslike TT Replicas, kept the name to the fore.

1930 596 cc Scott TT Replica

One of the best-loved British motorcycles of all time was the Yorkshire-built, two-stroke-twin, water-cooled Scott — as idiosyncratic a machine as the man from whom it took its name, Alfred Angas Scott. Based at Shipley, the Scott factory was an early supporter of the Isle of Man TT, winning in 1913 and 1914 (with rotary-inlet-valve models which were never put into general production) and gaining the manufacturers' team award in 1922.

Thereafter, though, racing success deserted the firm; but it didn't stop them from introducing, in 1929, the TT Replica model, in a choice of 498 or 596 cc capacities. Said the catalogue: 'Designed essentially for the speedman, the TT Replica is the outcome of years of racing experience. The engine has a longer stroke, and for power is in advance of any previous Scott engine. It is a replica of the machine finishing third in the 1928 Senior TT Race; in its design are embodied many original Scott features, and like all Scott machines it is built to an ideal. Its roadholding and cornering abilities are a revelation!'

In fact six machies had been entered for the 1928 Senior TT, powered by a new 498 cc longstroke engine (66.6 × 71.4 mm) housed in a short wheelbase frame in which the gearbox was brought closer to the engine. Tommy Hatch, a newcomer to the Isle of Man, was the man who brought his Scott home into third place, but the only other finisher of the squad was veteran Harry Langman, in twelfth spot.

Later in the year Langman was to lead the unlimited cc class of the Ulster Grand Prix for the first seven laps before retiring with engine trouble. Apart from enlarged oil and fuel tanks, and repositioning of the magneto to shorten the drive to it, the 1929 Scott official Senior TT entries were very much as before, and again the attack was six-handed. This time, however, the outcome was even more disappointing, and only Tommy Hatch finished the course, in no higher than thirteenth position.

The TT Replica continued into the 1930 programme, now featuring what was termed the Power-Plus engine; this featured an oil pump mounted on the crankcase door and driven by a disc from the overhung right-hand crankpin; provision was made for forcing oil direct to the big-end bearings. Cast-aluminium covers enclosed the final-drive sprocket on the near side, and the gearbox and magneto chain on the off side, so that the centre portion of the machine was almost entirely enclosed. The covers were each held by a single stud and nut, so that they could be detached readily for maintenance purposes.

Of Scott's own design, the front forks had best be described as 'Double-braced telescopic', a development of the simple telescopic type used by Scotts for many years, and these would continue to be specified for the 1931 TT Replica, changing for 1932 to Brampton Monarch girders.

A completely new design of Scott two-stroke twin was devised for the 1930 Senior TT, with the engine mounted vertically in the frame. Vibration problems early in the TT practice period meant that it was never raced and, instead, the riders reverted to the previous year's models. It was the last time the company was ever officially represented in the Isle of Man, and the projected production version of the vertical-engine Scott never materialized.

Specification

Make Scott. **Model** TT Replica. **Engine** 596 cc (74.6 × 68 mm) water-cooled two-stroke parallel twin. **Power output** 24 bhp at 5,000 rpm. **Tyres** 3.00 × 21 in front and rear. **Frame** Brazed-lug open-type tubular duplex. **Suspension** Undamped telescopic front forks. Rigid rear. **Weight** 335 lb dry. **Wheelbase** 54 in. **Manufacturer** The Scott Motor Cycle Co Ltd, Saltaire, Shipley, Yorkshire.

Above TT success had eluded the Scott works since their 1913 and 1914 victories so, said the catalogue, the 1930 TT Replica was based on the firm's 1928 third-place Senior TT entry. **Right** Though they lacked damping, telescopic front forks had been a Scott feature for many years. **Far right** The Scott engine employs a central flywheel and single-sided cranks, access to which is by way of circular crankcase doors retained by straps. **Below** The 'TT Rep' was among the most coveted of all Scott models, but there were plenty who mourned the passing of the simple two-speeder.

1923 493 cc Sunbeam 'George Dance' Sprinter

When it came to hurtling over a measured half-mile or mile in the shortest possible time, there was nobody to touch George Dance in the early 1920s. Soldered to the top of the fuel tank of the 493 cc Sunbeam sprinter displayed at the National Motorcycle Museum is a brass plate bearing the legend: "G. Dance, World and British Records, SM 78.26 mph, SK 71.97 mph'. Except, of course, that it is not just legend but the plain truth. On 31 October 1923, just before the Brooklands race track was due to close for its annual winter overhaul, George took the low and light Sunbeam to the new Standing Mile and Standing Kilometre records recorded on the plate.

He had joined the Sunbeam factory as a tester in April 1914, but it was soon apparent that he was, also, a born development engineer and when sprints and hill climbs resumed after World War 1 he became almost invincible on machines powered by engines he had himself converted from side-valve to overhead-valve operation. Incidentally, traffic on the public roads of the time was so light that the majority of sprints took place on the open highway.

Dance was involved in an alarming incident when, at an open hill climb near Newport, Gwent, in July of 1922 he missed the brake pedal at the conclusion of his run, went through a hedge, took off and landed in the branches of an apple tree! But at least he had already established his customary Fastest Time of the Day, and the run in which his mishap occurred (it was Event 13, significantly!) went down in the timekeeper's record as second fastest.

Comfort was one thing which George Dance tended to ignore, and it will be noted that the 'saddle' is nothing more than a leather cover over a metal pan, with no springing whatever. The extraordinarily wide handlebars were a George Dance trademark; he was a man of prodigious strength, and he needed it all to keep the machine in a straight line.

The engine of this particular machine is stamped 'EXP231' which can be interpreted as 'Experimental, 1923, No 1'. If that is indeed so, then this is the first overhead-valve engine to be produced officially by the Sunbeam factory (production versions would follow, in both 347 and 493 cc sizes, for the 1924 season). The company's designer was John E. Greenwood, but by that time Dance was the firm's Chief Development Engineer, in charge of the competitions and experimental shop, and responsible among other duties for preparation of the firm's TT entries.

George Dance himself raced occasionally, but his preference was for the straight-line stuff, in which he ranked as the George Brown of his day. Appropriately, he was among the entry when the very last open-road meeting of all took place in England, on the Hereford to Hay main road in 1925. Instead of bringing out his famous old machine he elected (perhaps on company instructions) to give the new Sunbeam overhead-camshaft model an airing. Not, though, with any degree of success.

He was again mounted on the overhead-camshaft model for his final public appearance of any kind, the 1925 Senior TT, but after working up to ninth place, he had to drop out on the fourth lap. It wasn't exactly the blaze of glory he might have preferred.

Specification

Make Sunbeam. **Model** 'George Dance' Sprinter. **Engine** 493 cc (80×98 mm bore and stroke) overhead-valve single. **Power output** Not quoted. **Tyres** 2.50×21 in front and rear. **Frame** Brazed-lug tubular diamond. **Suspension** Side-spring Druid girder front forks. Rigid rear. **Weight** 240 lb dry. **Wheelbase** 54 in. **Manufacturer** John Marston Ltd, Sunbeamland, Wolverhampton, Staffordshire.

74

Above The low build and thin wedge-shape fuel tank was typical of early-1920s sprint machines. Weight was pared to the bone.
Right Top sprint exponent of his day, George Dance insisted on very wide handlebars, his tremendous strength serving to keep the Sunbeam on a true path.
Far right Overhead-valve engines didn't enter the Sunbeam range until 1924, but this one is thought to be an experimental 1923 model.
Below Because a sprint dash lasted for a few seconds only, riding comfort could be largely ignored. This saddle is merely a leather-covered metal pan.

1934 493 cc Triumph 5/10

That Triumph should announce, in 1934, that they would be adding a series-production road racing model to their catalogue was a considerable surprise to enthusiasts of the period. True, in earlier years the Coventry concern had been involved in racing such machines as the four-valve Ricardo, and the two-valve Vic Horsman-devised TT model; but it had been six years since an official Triumph team had been seen in the Isle of Man races. *The Motor Cycle* confidently expected that the newcomer 'will beat the three-figure mark handsomely'; and they predicted also that a works Triumph squad would be contesting the 1934 Senior TT.

Yet on the face of it, the racing Triumph (catalogued as the Model 5/10) was nothing very special, for its power unit was essentially the Val Page-designed engine from the Mark 5 roadster — a two-valve, pushrod single that was destined to survive the 1936 takeover and continue, with Edward Turner cosmetic treatment, as the Tiger 90 until the coming of the immortal Speed Twin.

However the machine, said Triumph, was 'constructed to withstand prolonged periods of "all-out"', to which end the specification embraced 'high-grade forged disc flywheels, fitted with alloy-steel connecting rods (machined all over), and lightened reciprocating parts including tappets, pushrods and overhead rockers'. The same dry-sump lubrication system as employed on the roadster was fitted, though fed from a seven-pint oil tank and including an auxiliary feed to the rear of the cylinder.

Other fittings were a rubber racing saddle, foot gearchange, and (for Isle of Man use) a four-gallon fuel tank at £4 extra instead of the standard three-gallon item. Gear ratios could be close-ratio, or 'TT'. Wheel rims were of lightweight high-tensile steel, and brakes were 8 in at front and rear. Especially for the Model 5/10 was a completely new duplex tubular frame affording a lowered centre of gravity, with shortened front forks brazed up from tapered tubes.

And the factory was, it seemed, prepared to practice what they preached, for four machines were specially prepared for the Senior TT, the riders being Ernie Thomas, Jock West and Tommy Spann, with Allan Jefferies as a reserve rider understudying the official trio (which meant that Allan, too, had to take part in the practice period, in order to qualify himself). Team manager was Harry Perrey who, like Allan Jefferies, was primarily a trials kingpin.

Jefferies didn't actually take station on the starting grid, for practice had been uneventful, and the works teamsters all qualified as per programme. For Triumph, though, the race (run off in rain and heavy mist) was something of a disaster, with both Thomas and Spann dropping out with engine trouble in the early stages; Jock West skidded on the wet road at Ballacraine and dropped the bike, wiping off the right footrest. Eventually he was black-flagged and disqualified.

Many years later, what appeared to be a catalogue Model 5/10 turned up at an antique shop in Burton Latimer, Northamptonshire, and word was passed to Vintage MCC road-racer John Joiner. John already owned two spare Model 5/10 bottom-end assemblies, and the chance of a complete bike was too good to miss. A stripdown showed that, internally, a deal of skilled attention had been carried out. Suspecting that this was one of the 1934 works team bikes, he consulted Harry Perrey and, finally, it was confirmed that it was the 'spare' which had been used in the IoM practising by Allan Jefferies.

Specification

Make Triumph. **Model** 5/10. **Engine** 493 cc (84 × 89 mm bore and stroke) overhead-valve single. **Power output** 29 bhp at 5,800 rpm. **Tyres** 3.00 × 21 in front, 3.25 × 21 in rear. **Frame** Brazed-lug duplex cradle. **Suspension** Tubular girder front forks with friction dampers. Rigid rear. **Weight** 365 lb. **Wheelbase** 54 in. **Manufacturer** The Triumph Co Ltd, Priory Street, Coventry.

Above Though the Triumph factory turned against racing in Edward Turner days, in 1934 they catalogued a genuine road-race model (the 5/10) and, indeed, raced it themselves. **Right** All dressed up and nowhere to go, for the machine seen here was actually the 1934 works team reserve, rider Allan Jefferies. **Far right** Family resemblance between the 5/10's 493 cc engine, and the later Tiger 70, 80 and 90 singles is no coincidence. **Below** During 1934 TT practice in the Isle of Man, Jefferies dropped 'No 31' at Creg-ny-Baa, luckily without major damage. Mauve finish is correct.

1949 498 cc Triumph Grand Prix

Triumph chief Edward Turner was in no way racing oriented, and he had had no intention of introducing a series-production road-race model into the immediate post-World War 2 programme; but circumstances alter cases, and what led Turner to have a change of heart was the rather electrifying victory by Ernie Lyons, on a hybrid Triumph twin, in the 1946 Senior Manx Grand Prix.

This was the first post-war race to be held over the Isle of Man's famous TT circuit, and with the British motorcycle industry trying to struggle back into production in the face of countless restrictions on the supply of metals and other vital commodities, the field for the 1946 MGP was largely made up of pre-war machines and home-brewed specials.

But it so happened that among the wartime products of Triumph's recently-erected Meriden works had been a generator plant for the RAF, the engine unit of which was loosely based on that of the pre-war 498 cc Tiger 100. The lower assembly of the generator unit could not be adapted to motorcycle use; but the cylinder barrel and head were a very different matter because a primary consideration of the RAF order had been light weight and, accordingly, Triumphs had cast these items in a silicon-aluminium alloy.

In post-war Britain there was no light-alloy to spare for cylinder manufacture; but there were plenty of redundant RAF generators from which the barrels and heads could be stripped. So former Brooklands ace Freddie Clarke set to work to produce, for Ernie Lyons, a light and modern racer embodying a Tiger 100 lower assembly, topped by a light-alloy barrel and head fed by a pair of Amal carburettors.

Completing the assembly was a standard roadster frame (with the newly-announced Triumph telescopic front forks) and the prototype of a new rear wheel with self-contained springing — the latter a Turner dodge to avoid the expense of manufacturing new frame jigs for a rear-sprung model in the normal sense. An initial tryout in the Ulster Road Race was disappointing, for carburation bothers prevented it from showing its true potential; but in the Manx GP a few weeks later, held in a downpour, all went well — except that in the last few miles of the race the Triumph's front-down tube parted.

Such was the clamour from the elated public that Edward Turner relented to the extent of permitting a modest road-race development programme to be put in hand, with works support for Dave Whitworth (incidentally, the author's wartime commanding officer) in selected 1947 continental meetings.

From this there emerged, for the 1948 season, the Grand Prix. An initial batch of fifty was constructed, all using ex-generator barrels and heads, and nine of them were entered for the 1948 Senior TT. Seven started but, sad to say, all seven packed up; the sportster Tiger 100 bottom-end, it seemed, was not man enough for out-and-out racing. Nevertheless, further batches were made in the next couple of years, and it is believed about 200 were built in all. ('Of which', say the wisecrackers, 'about 350 have survived!' The Grand Prix has become one of the most popular and coveted of classic race models, and not all the survivors are genuine!)

Specification

Make Triumph. **Model** Grand Prix. **Engine** 498 cc (63 × 80 mm bore and stroke) overhead-valve vertical twin. **Power output** 40 bhp at 7,200 rpm. **Tyres** 3.00 × 20 in front, 3.50 × 19 in rear. **Frame** Brazed-lug and welded tubular cradle. **Suspension** Oil-damped telescopic front forks, sprung rear wheel hub. **Weight** 314 lb dry. **Wheelbase** 55 in. **Manufacturer** Triumph Engineering Co Ltd, Meriden Works, Allesley, Coventry.

Above The stuff of which legends are made, the Triumph Grand Prix began life as an alliance between the super-sports Tiger 100 — and a wartime generator engine. **Right** About 200 Grand Prix models were made and several can still be seen today in vintage races. **Far right** The square-finned silicon-alloy cylinder block, originally produced for the RAF airborne auxiliary generator, is readily recognizable by the two cast-in bosses between the fins. **Below** Triumph's glamorous Grand Prix in racing trim is guaranteed to bring 'Ooohs!' of appreciation from spectators everywhere!

1951 498 cc Triumph TR5 Trophy

Produced in rigid-frame form from 1949 to 1954 (and with swinging-arm rear suspension until 1958), Triumph's TR5 Trophy will be remembered with great affection by many readers as the 'last of the great all-rounders' — the bike you rode to work during the week but, at the weekend, could be trialled, grass-tracked, hill-climbed and even (on *very* short-circuits) road-raced with a fair chance of success. At least, that was true of the earlier rigid model, though with the advent of rear springing the TR5 lost some of its off-road agility and lightness of handling; by then, though, sport had become specialized and the day of the general-purpose competition model was passing.

Why the 'Trophy' name? That dates back to 1948, when the Triumph works were asked to provide four machines (and riders), as part of Britain's International Six-Days Trial national teams. Two of the four, ridden by Allan Jefferies (the team captain) and Jimmy Alves, formed part of our five-man squad challenging for the International Trophy (the lesser international competition was known as the Vase). The British team was successful, and the Triumph works dubbed their new production competition model the Trophy, in recognition.

However, it wasn't quite that simple, for at the time Triumph works trials riders were using lightened versions of the 350 cc 3T twin, and these were not thought suitable for the ISDT squad. So the Meriden competition department had to build some 'specials' — basically rigid-frame Speed Twins but with the silicon-alloy square-finned cylinder block and head of the wartime generator unit (we met that before, when considering the Triumph Grand Prix) disguised so far as was possible with a lick of black paint.

At the same time that the TR5 Trophy was put into production for the 1949 season, Triumph were building the side-valve TRW vertical twin for military purposes, and it was fortuitous that the Trophy could make use of the TRW's short-wheelbase frame. The crankcase assembly was basically Tiger 100, but with a rather milder camshaft, and the upper works were those of the wartime generator unit — no longer camouflaged with black paint, but presented in their sand-cast nakedness.

A siamesed exhaust system on the left ran at modestly high level, and was both practical (permitting the machine to ford quite deep streams) and stylish. Shortened mudguards provided more clearance than usual, to prevent the wheels becoming clogged in muddy going.

Presumably the supply of generator-plant cylinder blocks had dried up by 1951, for that season saw the advent of a new close-finned, die-cast light-alloy block, adopted also by the sports-roadster Tiger 100, and the outcome was perhaps the most aesthetically pleasing competitions machine of all time. For three years in succession, Triumph gained the ISDT manufacturers' team award, for the TR5 was in its element in long-distance competition; it was, too, a favourite with those adventurous types who would leave the highway and go exploring mountain tracks.

But as the 1950s ran on, the lack of proper rear springing (the optional Triumph Sprung Hub was only marginally effective, in addition to making the machine tail-heavy) was becoming noticeable, and though a swinging-arm was added from 1955 the heyday of the TR5 was already over, and the later model never achieved the same following.

Specification

Make Triumph. **Model** TR5 Trophy. **Engine** 498 cc (63 × 80 mm bore and stroke) overhead-valve vertical twin. **Power output** 25 bhp at 6,000 rpm. **Tyres** 3.00 × 20 in front, 4.00 × 19 in rear. **Frame** All-welded tubular cradle type. **Suspension** Oil-damped telescopic front forks. Rigid rear frame, but wheel incorporates Triumph Sprung Hub. **Weight** 304 lb dry. **Wheelbase** 53 in. **Manufacturer** Triumph Engineering Co Ltd, Meriden Works, Allesley, Coventry.

Above Rare among post-war machines, the TR5 Trophy was a true all-round competitions model, at home in most forms of motor cycle sport. **Right** High-level Siamese exhaust pipes add to the TR5's sense of purpose; headlamp was quickly detachable. **Far right** Initially, TR5 cylinder blocks were of sand-cast silicon alloy, but from 1951 on there was a new light-alloy die casting with precision close-pitch finning. **Below** Pretty as a picture, but businesslike, too, the Trophy's name reflected Britain's Trophy team success in the 1948 International Six-Days Trial.

1955 649 cc Triumph Thunderbird 'Johnny Allen Record Breaker'

The dried-out bed of a salt-water lake, Bonneville Salt Flats are in the state of Utah, USA. Vast and featureless, they form the only possible location for a world speed record attempt — but even so the flats are only firm enough for such a purpose in August and early September. Miss your chance, and you would have to wait for almost a year for the surface to become dry and hard again.

For several years Bonneville had been the scene of an annual speed festival, but in August of 1955 a machine appeared, the like of which had not been seen before. Designed by an aircraft pilot named Stormy Mangham and powered by a much-modified 649 cc Triumph Thunderbird engine, it was a long, low cigar-shaped projectile in which the driver sat ahead of the engine. Orginally, Mangham himself was to have driven it, but he felt it would be 'too fast for owner' so, instead, a 26-year-old Texan named Johnny Allen (who had been running Triumph machines owned by Pete Dalio and tuned by Jack Wilson) volunteered for the hot seat.

Running on alcohol fuel, and with a top gear of 2.5 to 1 — which, in theory, should have returned a speed of 220 mph at 7,000 rpm — Allen returned flying-kilometre and flying-mile mean speeds of 193.72 and 192.308 mph respectively. The timekeeper was Bus Schaller and the figures were given official recognition as being American national speed records, though they were rejected by the Federation Internationale Motorcycliste because neither the timekeeper nor his apparatus had been given prior FIM approval.

The following year, when the Bonneville salt again reached a suitable state, Germany's NSU factory made a bid for the world record, with Wilhelm Herz establishing a new all-time high of 211 mph. Yet no sooner had the NSU team left the scene than back came Stormy Mangham, Pete Dalio, Jack Wilson and, of course, Johnny Allen. In the interim, at his Fort Worth workshop, tuner Jack Wilson had been extracting still more power from the 649 cc iron-head-and-barrel Thunderbird engine.

It was still unsupercharged, but was fed by two 1⅛ in Amal carburettors and ran at 12 to 1 compression ratio.

This time the timekeeper was Art Spilsbury, and the record-attempt team had been assured that both Spilsbury and his time equipment were acceptable to the FIM. So on 6 September, 1956, the 'flying cigar' whistled down the salt and through the measured distances, to produce a mean speed of 214.4 mph for the flying mile.

Johnny Allen had set a new world record; hadn't he? At first it seemed so, for the FIM despatched a telegram signifying their acceptance of the figure. But at the FIM Congress, president Piet Nortier dropped a bombshell. The NSU company, apparently, were querying the validity of the figures, of the timekeeper, and of the timing apparatus. In the circumstances, said Nortier, the FIM was withdrawing their confirmation.

Infuriated, the Triumph company, on Allen's behalf, instituted legal proceedings against the FIM, and for two years the case dragged through the international courts. At length Edward Turner, fed up with the whole affair, backed out. So the FIM never did give Johnny's 214.4 mph official standing. But in the eyes of the motorcyclists everywhere it *was* a record...

Specification

Make Triumph. **Model** Thunderbird special. **Engine** 649 cc (71 × 82 mm bore and stroke) overhead-valve vertical twin. **Power output** Not disclosed; claimed by USA to be around 80 bhp, but more likely 65 bhp. **Tyres** 3.00 × 19 in front and rear. **Frame** All-welded space frame, incorporating parts of original Triumph Thunderbird frame. **Suspension** Oil-damped telescopic front forks. Swinging-arm rear forks controlled by rubber bands. **Weight** Not disclosed. **Wheelbase** 112 in. **Manufacturer** Triumph Engineering Co Ltd, Meriden Works, Allesley, Coventry.

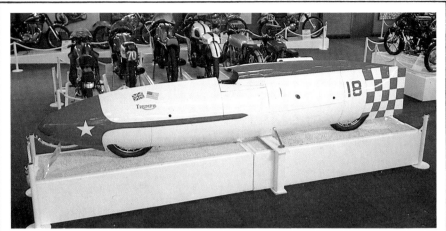

Above In the long and lean cigar-like fuselage, the driver sat amidships, ahead of the engine. Designer of the shell was Stormy Mangham. **Right** A semi-frontal view illustrates the wind-cheating nature of the slim and smooth bodywork. A detachable cowling shields the driver's head. **Far right** Access to the 649 cc engine is by a hatch in the right-hand side. The cast-iron Thunderbird engine is fed by twin Amal carburettors. **Below** Flags of the USA and Britain adorn the nose of the Johnny Allen special. Allen's success gave Triumph their most enduring model name — the Bonneville.

1970 741 cc Triumph Trident T150 'Slippery Sam'

It is given to very few motorcycles to become legends in their own lifetime; one can think of 'Copperknob' of 'Nero', of 'Old Bill', and perhaps one or two more — and, of course, there is 'Slippery Sam', the only machine in the history of powered two-wheeling to have won five 750 cc Production Machine TT races in five successive years.

Nor is that all, for Sam was the first production bike to win a TT at over 100 mph, twice winner of the Silverstone production-machine race, and a consistent runner in such events as the Bol d'Or and the Hutchinson 100. In fact, it was in one of the Bol d'Or events (over the famed Le Mans circuit in France) that the Triumph earned the 'Slippery Sam' nickname; despite a lubrication system failure, it ran home in fifth place, liberally coated in oil.

Sam began life as one of three Model T150 Tridents hand-built in the Triumph competitions department at Meriden for the works team in the 1970 750 cc Isle of Man Production-machine TT. The riders would be Malcolm Uphill (twice a winner of the event on Triumph Bonnevilles), Paul Smart, and Tom Dickie and, as indeed they had to be to conform to the regulations of the event, the trio of three-cylinder models were to standard production specification apart from a very few permitted modifications.

By chance, it was Tom Dickie who was allocated the machine which would become known as Sam, and Tom had a relatively comfortable ride to finish fourth while Uphill, on another of the trio, claimed the winner's laurels; the third Trident, that of Paul Smart, went out with a flat front tyre while leading.

For 1971, 'Slippery Sam' was again works-entered for the Production TT, with Ray Pickrell aboard. It gave Ray an outright win, and thus the legend began. But now Triumph-BSA were running into financial trouble, the competitions department closed down and Sam was sold — luckily to Triumph development engineer, Les Williams.

There would be no more works entries, but when Pickrell needed a bike for the 1972 Production race, Les offered the Trident, personally prepared it for the meeting and rode it up to Liverpool to catch the steamer. Ray won for the second time, and thereafter it became accepted practice that to win the Isle of Man Production event, one had merely to borrow 'Slippery Sam' from Les and — like Red Rum and the Grand National — it knew its own way round the course. Sam's third successive win, in 1973, was for Tony Jefferies; its fourth, in 1974, was for Mick Grant.

For 1975 there was a change of format for the race, the length being extended to a gruelling ten laps (377 miles) and the saddle being shared by two riders. It made no difference. Said the *Motor Cycle's* headline: 'Play It Again, Sam!' Sam obliged, bringing victory to the pairing of Dave Croxford and Alex George and lifting the lap record to 102.88 mph.

But 'Slippery Sam' was absent from the 1976 event, the organizers having ruled that at six years old it was, maybe, getting a little long in the tooth. Phooey, said Triumph fans everywhere, they just wanted to let someone else have a chance of winning...

Specification

Make Triumph. **Model** Trident T150. **Engine** 741 cc (67 × 70 mm bore and stroke) overhead-valve three cylinder with cranks at 120 degrees. **Power output** 58 bhp at 7,250 rpm. **Tyres** 3.25 × 19 in front, 4.10 × 19 in rear. **Frame** All-welded tubular cradle. **Suspension** Oil-damped telescopic front forks. Swinging arm rear forks controlled by spring and hydraulic units. **Weight** 468 lb dry. **Wheelbase** 58 in. **Manufacturer** Triumph Engineering Co Ltd, Meriden Works, Allesley, Coventry.

Above Worshipped by Triumph fans as the most illustrious machine ever built at Meriden, 'Slippery Sam' notched up five consecutive 750 cc Production-machine TT victories and was (among other glories) the first model to win the race at over 100 mph. **Right** Underneath the sleek racing fairing, Sam is a standard Trident T150 at heart — but meticulously prepared by owner Les Williams. **Far right** With delightful road manners, the machine was in fact *ridden* to the Isle of Man for the 1972 TT meeting — and won! **Below** Very distinctive, the triple-outlet 'ray gun' silencers were specially designed.

1912 976 cc Trump-JAP '90 Bore'

The casual passer-by may very well misread the 'Trump' name on the tank of the formidable-looking veteran racing model displayed here as the better-known 'Triumph'; but in fact Trump was an independent make with a most honourable Brooklands heritage. Francis McNab (who, incidentally, was to be one of the founder committee members of the Vintage Motor Cycle Club in 1946) was the originator of Trump, the first of which was built in makeshift premises at Liphook, Hampshire, circa 1906. However, with the opening of the famous Brooklands track McNab recruited his cousin, Angus Maitland, and the firm of Trump Motors Ltd was formed, with a factory adjacent to the circuit at Byfleet, Surrey.

Colonel R. N. Stewart — whose wife Gwenda, sister of Glubb Pasha of the Jordan Arab Legion, was a Brooklands record-breaker in her own right — was brought in as managing director; and since McNab, Maitland and Colonel Stewart were all prominent on Trump-JAP machines in the early Brooklands days, the firm also maintained a shed and workshop in the paddock area where their race bikes were kept and fettled.

Francis McNab, in particular, made sure that Trump gained plenty of publicity. As early as 1909 he established a British 500 cc one-hour record by covering 48 miles 400 yards, and a year later he was the victor in a special handicap race, on a 482 cc Trump-JAP, against a Farman biplane piloted by Blondeau, a French aviation pioneer. 1911 saw him as the first man to cover 60 miles in an hour on a 500 cc, and later he same year he set up a new two-hour record of 110 miles and a record average of 55 mph for a hundred miles.

With bore and stroke dimensions of 90 × 77.5 mm, the new vertical-valve ohv racing J. A. Prestwich engines were new for the 1911 season, and came in single (488 cc) and vee-twin (976 cc) form. Both McNab and Stewart immediately fitted the single-cylinder

version into Trump frames, while Charlie Collier used the vee-twin in the Matchless with which he contested a three-leg match race at Brooklands against American ace, Jake de Rosier.

Also in 1911, Trump Motors moved house again, this time to Birmingham where they established a factory in Lombard Street, and offices in John Bright Street. Their advertisements claimed: 'All machines maufactured by Trump Motors are built under the supervision of director and sales manager F. A. McNab, and are personally tested by him.' However, both Maitland and McNab had left the firm by 1913, and the business continued under the direction of Colonel Stewart (his wife Gwenda also retained a financial interest, as did Colonel Janson who was to be her second husband). After World War 1, some racing models were still made, including an eight-valve Trump-Anzani twin for Stewart, but the output by then was mainly of Peco-engined utility two-strokes, the 'last Trump' being sounded in 1923.

Owned and raced in post-World War 2 years by the late John Griffith, the particular Trump-JAP '90 Bore' twin illustrated is thought to have been used until Guy Fawkes' Day, 1921, by Colonel Stewart, his outings thereafter being on the eight-valve Trump-Anzani. The additional oil tank above the top tube of the frame was for use in long-distance racing.

Specification

Make Trump. **Model** '90 Bore'. **Engine** JAP 976 cc (90 × 77.5 mm bore and stroke) vertical-valve overhead valve vee-twin. **Power output** Not quoted. **Tyres** 650 × 65 mm, front and rear, beaded edge. **Frame** Brazed-lug tubular diamond. **Suspension** Druid side-spring girder front forks. Rigid at rear. **Weight** Not quoted. **Wheelbase** 55 in. **Manufacturer** Trump Motors Ltd, John Bright Street (works Lombard Street), Birmingham.

Above The majority of Trump motorcycles were specifically built to customer's requirements, at workshops adjoining the famous Brooklands race track. **Right** High-built front forks bely the competitive nature of the 1912 Trump-JAP. Extra oil tank, above the fuel tank, was for use in long-distance racing. **Far right** The 90 mm bore, vertical valve ohv engine was a 1911 introduction by JAP of Tottenham; valve gear is completely exposed. **Below** Straight-through exhaust pipes, for this was before the days of the 'Brooklands Can'. Trump production ended in 1923.

1961 499 cc Velocette Venom 24-hour Record Breaker

Perhaps you're right; it doesn't look as glamorous as all that. Just a well-used standard roadster, you reckon? But that is exactly right — a standard 499 cc Velocette Venom Clubman, taken from stock and carefully tuned, fitted with the ordinary roadster Veeline dolphin fairing from the factory's own catalogue, then well-used by being hammered around and around the bumpy 1½-mile concrete bowl known as Montlhéry Autodrome, just outside Paris, for 24 hours.

And the outcome? World 12-hour and 24-hour records in the 500, 750 and 1,000 cc solo classes, at average speeds of 104.66 mph for the shorter time and 100.05 mph for the longer. Which is a pretty fantastic performance for a good old British pushrod single with a long-in-the-tooth design dating right back to 1934!

The Velocette factory had spent several months prior to the record attempt tuning the Venom to produce the necessary torque, power and (of course) stamina until it was pushing out 39.8 bhp at a peak — a plateau, more like — of 5,500 to 5,900 rpm. How that was done was not disclosed, but certainly the 1 3/16 in Amal Grand Prix carburettor was being run as rich as possible. Top gear was raised from the standard 4.87 to 1, to 3.98 to 1 by substituting a 22-tooth final-drive sprocket for the normal 18-tooth one, and that meant that it was able to lap steadily at 110 to 112 mph.

For the Montlhéry expedition a team of eight riders was recruited, of which two (Velocette sales director Bertie Goodman, and journalist Bruce Main-Smith) were British, while the remaining six were French and were headed by veteran racer and record-breaker Georges Monneret. But don't imagine a billiard-table track. As Bruce Main-Smith was to comment: 'Montlhéry is a bowl-shaped, concrete-banked slice of medieval punishment. It has two minute straights and two torture-inflicting pieces of bump-infested purgatory described as high-speed bankings.

On this anti-clockwise course is painted a yellow medial line which is the offical distance. One must not go below this according to the regulations.

'In fact, at 110 mph the line is about the lowest point of the banking at which to ride, and during the actual attempt most pilots were about a yard-and-a-half higher to avoid the bumpier track lower down. One is then too high and stays up by leaning over to the right (relative to the banking) which unfortunately hastens tyre wear.'

For the first dozen hours things went relatively smoothly, except that during the first hour Georges Monneret came in for an unexpected stop, having misinterpreted the enthusiastic waving of a bystander for a pit signal. But real trouble came after the 12-hour record was safely in the bag, when it was discovered that a rivet had sheared in the gear-change mechanism. The machine was flagged in for examination and repair, the latter being done with all speed. Nevertheless, during the time the Venom was stationary the clock was ticking on, and the overall average speed had dropped below the magic 'ton'. Not until the final hour of running did it creep upward and, at last, pass the 100 mph figure.

Specification

Make Velocette. **Model** Venom. **Engine** 499 cc (86 × 86 mm bore and stroke) overhead-valve single. **Power output** 39.8 bhp at 5,500 rpm. **Tyres** 3.00 × 19 in front, 3.25 × 19 in rear. **Frame** Brazed-lug tubular cradle. **Suspension** Oil-damped telescopic front forks. Swinging-arm rear forks controlled by spring-and-hydraulic units. **Weight** 375 lb dry. **Wheelbase** 54 in. **Manufacturer** Veloce Ltd, Hall Green Works, York Road, Birmingham 28.

Above To maintain a 100 mph-plus average for 24 hours was a remarkable achievement by what was basically a standard Velocette Venom roadster. Power output was fractionally under 40 bhp. **Right** It wasn't even a road-racing fairing! The streamlining is actually the firm's catalogued Veeline dolphin with the headlamp aperture blanked off. **Far right** Glass-fibre side shields hide the engine, but the 1 3/16 in Amal Grand Prix carburettor is visible. **Below** Velocette styling, and engine design, changed but little over the years and the 1961 Venom's 1934 ancestry is very apparent.

1967 499 cc Velocette Thruxton Venom

Ever since there were tracks to race on, manufacturers have named particular models in honour of successes gained — or, maybe, in the hope that successes would be gained — at particular venues. Look at the number of 'TT' or 'Brooklands' models there have been over the years. And Thruxton? Well, that is the name of an airfield circuit not far from Andover, Hampshire, where a very popular series of production-machine marathons was held in the 1950 and 1960s.

Except that certain modifications could be made in the interests of safety, machines entered for the Thruxton 500-Miler had to be as per the maker's catalogue; and so that a competitor shouldn't drop out through sheer exhaustion, every competing machine was shared by a pair of alternating riders.

This type of racing was especially suitable for the big 499 cc Velocette singles, and the success of the standard Venom in earlier events led to the 1964 introduction of a high-performance kit which incorporated a new cylinder head with downdraught inlet tract and an Amal GP carburettor, a larger-diameter inlet valve, and modified valve angles.

The kit, however, was just an interim measure, and 1965 saw the coming of the first Venom Thruxton. Not only did this model have all the goodies previously offered in the high-performance kit, but there was a racy-looking seat with humped back so that the flat-down-to-it rider wouldn't slide over the back, plus rear-set footrests and associated controls.

And wouldn't you just know it, that no sooner had Velocette produced the Venom Thruxton than the organizers vacated the Thruxton track, to stage the 1965 500-Miler on a completely different circuit at Castle Combe, Wiltshire. Not that it made much difference, for after two other Velocettes had taken turns at leading the 500 cc class, a third example (shared by Joe Dunphy and David Dixon) came home as the winner.

The Venom Thruxton which is a proud member of the National Motorcycle Museum collection dates from 1967, and is particularly smart with its navy-blue frame and blue-finished seat contrasting with the gold-lined silver of the racing tank. That year, the 500-Miler moved to Brand's Hatch, and for much of the period it seemed likely that Velocette would again take the 500 cc honours. With one hour of race time left, the Thruxton Venom of Reg Everett and Tom Phillips was holding an eight-laps clear advantage over its nearest rival — but then it stopped, out of sparks.

However, in the same year the Isle of Man TT series included the first production-machine TT, and there Neil Kelly and Keith Heckles more than made up for the Brands Hatch disappointment by finishing first and second in the 500 cc class. Yet for all its track-racing prowess, the Thruxton Venom remained a thoroughly practical road-going model, notwithstanding the 2 in-diameter inlet valve and Amal GP carburettor, and on road test returned the remarkable fuel consumption figure of 58 mpg at 70 mph! Remaining in production to the end of the Velocette factory's existence, it was the culmination of years of development of the high-camshaft, single-cylinder engine that had entered the company's range as long ago as 1934.

Specification

Make Velocette. **Model** Thruxton Venom. **Engine** 499 cc (86 × 86 mm bore and stroke) overhead-valve single. **Power output** 41 bhp at 6,250 rpm. **Tyres** 3.00 × 19 in front, 3.25 × 19 in rear. **Frame** Brazed-lug tubular cradle. **Suspension** Oil-damped telescopic front forks. Swinging-arm rear forks controlled by spring-and-hydraulic units, adjustable for angle to suit varying loads. **Weight** 375 lb dry. **Wheelbase** 53.75 in. **Manufacturer** Veloce Ltd, Hall Green Works, York Road, Hall Green, Birmingham 28.

Above Traditional Velocette finish was black with rich gold lining, but the Thruxton Venom broke new ground by appearing in eye-catching blue and silver. **Right** A John Tickle product, the twin-leading-shoe front brake in a full-width hub was hi-tech stuff by the standards of the day! **Far right** Velocette's high-camshaft/short-pushrod engine design stood the test of time, for its ancestry went back to 1934. **Below** The Thruxton name honoured the airfield circuit near Andover, home of the long-distance races in which Velocettes so often dominated the 500 cc class.

1949 998 cc Vincent-HRD Series C Black Lightning

Among motorcycle clubmen of the relatively immediate post-war years, the Black Lightning was the one whispered about with reverant awe. After all, wasn't it the first-ever machine to be ridden at more than 150 mph — only *just* over the ton-and-a-half, but nonetheless... In fact it was America's Rollie Free who set that 150.313 mph figure (an American national record) on Bonneville Salt Flats, Utah in September of 1948. Not only was the bike naked and unblown, but Rollie himself wore nothing but a pair of swimming trunks and trainer shoes, lying prone on the machine with his feet sticking out beyond the rear mudguard.

For good measure, in the same week Belgium's René Milhoux, with another Black Lightning, got the Belgian standing-start mile and kilometre sidecar records at 83.5 and 94 mph respectively then, discarding the chair, snaffled the Belgian solo record at 143.2 mph.

Those speed attempts, duly recorded in the weekly motorcycle press, were the first intimation that the British public had received that there *was* such a model as the Black Lightning. But the Earls Court Show was fast coming up, and when the doors were opened, there was a Black Lightning taking pride of place on the Vincent-HRD stand.

Billed as an export-only, out-and-out racer and sold without lighting equipment but with straight-through pipes, light-alloy wheel rims and a pair of 1 3/16 in TT Amal carburettors, it was priced at £508—£108 more than the sports-roadster Black Shadow twin from which it had been derived. That was *real* money, at a time when an alloy-engined Ariel Square Four would have set you back no more than £228, and a race-ready KTT Velocette was listed at £340.

The Black Lightning was 'Black' because its crankcases and timing covers were stove-enamelled that shade while the barrels and heads were black-anodized, and 'Lightning' because that was what it went like. Indeed, only a short while before the Earls Court Show opened, George Brown had taken a Lightning to third place in the Dunholme 100-Mile 1,000 cc Race; and that was darned good going, because the two machines that finished ahead of him were works AJS Porcupine twins.

The 'Series C' designation indicated that the Lightning, like other models in the 1949 range, was equipped with Vincent's new and patented Girdraulic front forks. As the name implied, these were girder-type forks (except that the side blades were not tubular fabrications but heat-treated light-alloy forgings), assisted by hydraulic damper units disposed behind each blade.

Ostensibly in production from 1948 to 1954, the Black Lightning was built in very limited numbers only, but in addition to those already mentioned, one other example was to feature in the record books. The date was July 1955, when New Zealand enthusiasts Russel Wright and Bob Burns enclosed an unblown Lightning in a home-built fairing and, on a narrow and bumpy road near Christchurch, New Zealand, established new world's-fastest records in the solo and sidecar classes at 185.15 and 163.06 mph respectively. A year later, Bob Burns was to push the sidecar figure still further, to 176 mph at Bonneville, but in a sense that was a requiem for the make.

Specification

Make Vincent—HRD. **Model** Black Lightning. **Engine** 998 cc (84×90 mm bore and stroke) overhead-valve vee-twin. **Power output** 70 bhp at 5,600 rpm. **Tyres** 3.00×21 in front, 3.50×20 in rear. **Frame** None. Engine suspended from backbone which is also the oil tank. **Suspension** Girder front forks, assisted by hydraulic damping struts. Cantilever rear springing, with spring and damper units under seat. **Weight** 380 lb dry. **Wheelbase** 56.5 in. **Manufacturer** The Vincent-HRD Co Ltd, Great North Road, Stevenage, Hertfordshire.

Above Highest-tuned (and rarest) of all Vincent-HRD models, the Black Lightning was a pure racing model capable of 150 mph. **Right** Distinguishing the Series C machines are the unique Girdraulic front forks, in which heat-treated light-alloy girder blades are assisted by separate hydraulic damper units. **Far right** The characteristic black-finish power unit was obtained by stove-enamelling the crankcase and timing cover, and black-anodizing the cylinder barrels and heads. **Below** Straight-through exhaust pipes, light-alloy wheel rims, and Amal TT carburettors were all part of the imposing specification.

1951 499 cc Vincent Series C Grey Flash

Marketed in 1950 and 1951 only, the single-cylinder Vincent Grey Flash was, to quote *Motor Cycling*, 'a Comet produced to Black Lightning standards' and it was listed in a choice of three options. At £349 5s, it came stripped for racing; at £368 6s it was supplied with full road-going equipment; but at £381 it was available fully equipped 'but with all the extras necessary for stripping and preparing for racing', those extras comprising a straight-through exhaust pipe, alternative sprockets and a rev-counter.

To explain further, the Comet was the Vincent-HRD company's post-war touring single and was, in essence, the front cylinder of the better-known vee-twin. Black Lightning-standard race preparation, however, meant enlarging, streamlining and polishing the cylinder head ports; fitting triple valve springs, lightening and polishing the 85 ton nickel-chrome steel conrod and the flywheels, and giving the rockers and cam followers the same treatment.

Announced late in 1949, the Grey Flash carried the factory's hopes for the 1950 Senior TT, in which no fewer than five of the new models were entered, with George Brown (later supplanted by Ken Bills), Johnny Hodgkin, and Manliff Barrington among the riders. With drilled frame and specially lightened front forks, and a 32 mm Amal TT carburettor, the racing Flash weighed in at under 300 lb.

But there were disturbing reports from the early TT practice periods, where the Burman gearboxes had been giving trouble, and a switch was made to boxes of Albion manufacture for the race. Even more alarming was the failure of an experimental big-end bearing arrangement, and though Ken Bills was to finish the 1950 Senior in twelfth position, the only other finisher was private owner F. Fairburn — 51st and second-last.

Back on the mainland, Johnny Hodgkin, and teenager John Surtees (a £5-a-week apprentice at the Vincent factory) kept the Grey Flash in the hunt, but it was not really good enough for the job. As Surtees was to recall: 'The Flash could cope with the old Garden Gate Norton, but when Norton started to sell the Featherbed Manx I realized the days of the Flash were numbered'.

The machine exhibited in the National Motorcycle Museum collection is one of the last of the 1951 batch and, as such, represents the ultimate stage of development. Learning from their TT experience, Vincent had by now adopted as standard the Albion Model H racing gearbox and five-plate clutch. But it would seem that they had lost faith in their own product so far as the TT was concerned, and the sole Grey Flash in the 1951 Senior was ridden by Johnny Hodgkin — and he retired at Glentramman on the last lap, without every having been anywhere in the reckoning.

All the same, it would be a mistake to write off the Grey Flash as a dud. It knocked up quite a respectable total of honours in minor races abroad; and young John Surtees gave the great Geoff Duke a run for his money in a pouring-wet ACU 'Festival of Britain' meeting at Thruxton (everything had a 'Festival of Britain' label in 1951). It's just that the competition was just a bit too strong for it — and that not everyone had the inbred ability of a Surtees.

Specification

Make Vincent. **Model** Grey Flash. **Engine** 499 cc (84 × 90 mm bore and stroke) overhead-valve single. **Power output** 35 bhp at 6,200 rpm. **Tyres** 3.00 × 21 in front, 3.50 × 20 in rear. **Frame** None in the conventional sense, the engine being suspended from a backbone member which is also the oil tank. **Suspension** Vincent Girdraulic girder front forks with hydraulic damping struts. Cantilever rear springing controlled by spring units and hydraulic damper under seat. **Weight** 330 lb dry. **Wheelbase** 55.75 in. **Manufacturer** The Vincent-HRD Co Ltd, Great North Road, Stevenage, Hertfordshire.

Above Though pre-war Vincent-HRD singles mounted the engine in an upright position, the post-war counterparts were virtually vee-twins with the rear cylinder missing! **Right** Vincent's Series C front forks were unique, with heat-treated-alloy blades in tandem with long and slim damper units. **Far right** Unique, too, was the Vincent valve gear; forked-end rocker arms operated each valve between upper and lower valve guides. **Below** Other Vincent models used gearboxes of the company's own design, but the Grey Flash employed a racing-pattern Albion. Stripped, the machine could reach 115 mph.

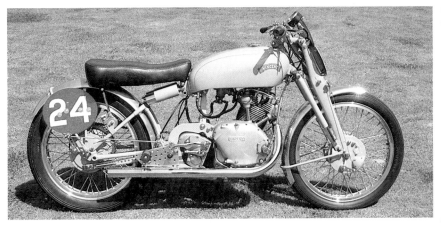

The National Motorcycle Museum

The world's only purpose-built museum complex expressly devoted to the history of the British-built motorcycle, the National Motorcycle Museum at Bickenhill — directly opposite the main entrance to the National Exhibition Centre, and right on the junction of the M42 Motorway and A45 Birmingham-Coventry trunk road — is a dream come to reality. The dreamer was Birmingham businessman Roy Richards (now the Museum's Founding Trustee), a motorcycle enthusiast who was disappointed that existing museums, with their handlebar-to-handlebar dusty and soulless line-ups, were no way to show the coming generation the kind of machines which thronged the roads in Dad's (or maybe Granddad's) day.

No, there should be a bright and airy building in which each machine would be shown to best advantage; and the machines themselves should be in sparkling, showroom condition, restored to virtually brand-new order by the best workmen available — if possible, by former employees of the factories which built the models in the first place.

Sadly, between the time that Roy Richards started his campaign to collect and restore the several hundreds of motorcycles necessary, and the eventual opening of the Museum premises, the once-dominant British two-wheel industry had shrunk to a mere shadow of its former self. But he pressed on undaunted, by now heading a charitable trust set up to administer the Museum's affairs. Fund-raising was hard work — indeed it still is, for the intention is to expand both the premises and the collection as circumstances allow — but the outcome is, as Roy had dreamed so many years ago, a true Mecca for enthusiasts, the world's finest exhibition of the British motorcycle in all its many forms.

Tree Trips
- Wide Wonderful World

Perjalanan Pohon
-Dunia Indah yang Luas

May we travel widely, to experience the earth's many wonders!

Mari kita berpergian secara luas, untuk mengalami banyak keindahan dunia.

Table of Contents

Daftar Isi

iii

An apple tree grows in the green countryside near a road.

Sebatang pohon apel tumbuh di pedesaan yang hijau dekat suatu jalan.

1

Everyday, the tree sees people in cars driving by. It wonders where are they going in such a hurry.

Setiap hari, pohon itu melihat orang di dalam mobil yang sedang melewatinya. Pohon merasa heran, ke mana mereka akan pergi terlihat begitu terburu- buru.

2

One day, a car stops. The people jump out of the car. They take pictures of the tree.

Suatu hari, sebuah mobil berhenti. Orang-orang meloncat keluar dari mobil. Mereka mengambil gambar pohon itu.

3

Tree asks the people, "Where
are you driving to in such a hurry?"

Pohon bertanya kepada orang itu, "Kemana kamu
akan mengemudikan mobil dengan terburu- buru
seperti itu?"

4

"We live in the city. We work there too." say the people.

"Kami tinggal di kota. Kami juga bekerja di sana." Kata orang tersebut.

Tree asks, "What is the city like?"

The people explain, "There are tall buildings in the city. At night, there are rainbows of bright lights also."

Pohon bertanya, "Seperti apakah kota itu?"

Orang itu menjelaskan, "Banyak gedung- gedung tinggi di kota. Pada malam hari, ada banyak pelangi dari lampu- lampu yang cerah."

6

7

The people continue, "There are lots of things to do too like movies, restaurants and malls." Tree replies, "I would like to visit the city."

Orang itu melanjutkan, "Ada banyak hal yang dilakukan seperti nonton film, makan di restauran, dan pergi ke mal. Pohon menyahut, "Aku ingin mengunjungi kota itu."

8

The people say, "Well, if you make it to the city, you can stay with us."

Orang itu mengatakan, "Baiklah, kalau kamu bisa pergi ke kota, kamu bisa tinggal bersama kami."

9

"Hmmm?" said the tree as it looks at its roots stuck in the ground. Tree thinks and thinks about what to do. It Googles for ideas. Finally, tree has an "Ahaa!" moment.

"Hmmm?" kata pohon yang akar-akarnya menancap di tanah. Pohon berpikir dan berpikir tentang apa-apa yang akan dilakukan. Pohon itu mencari ide di Google. Akhirnya, pohon itu mempunyai satu momen, "Ahaa!"

10

Tree sells its apples to get money.

Pohon itu menjual apelnya
untuk mendapatkan uang.

11

Tree has a special trolley made.
Workers with a special digger crane
help lift the tree into the trolley.

Pohon itu mempunyai satu trem buatan yang
istimewa. Para pekerja dengan derek penggali
khusus, membantu mengangkat pohon ke dalam trem.

Tree goes to the city and visits its friends. Good thing they have a big enough space where tree can stay.

Pohon itu pergi ke kota dan mengunjungi teman temannya. Bagusnya, mereka mempunyai satu ruang yang cukup besar di mana pohon bisa tinggal.

13

The people take the tree on a tour of the city.
Tree sees the tall buildings, shopping malls and
centers. At night, tree sees the bright many
colored lights.

Orang membawa pohon itu ke wisata kota. Pohon itu
melihat gedung- gedung tinggi, mal, dan pusat-pusat
perbelanjaan. Pada malam hari, pohon itu melihat lampu
warna-warni yang gemerlap.

14

Tree thinks that the city is interesting. There are lots of glass and steel and concrete but...

Pohon berpikir bahwa kota itu menarik...
Ada banyak kaca, baja dan beton, tetapi...

15

Tree notices there aren't any plants.

Pohon mencermati tidak
ada tumbuh- tumbuhan.

16

Tree helps the people plant lots of plants in the city.

Pohon membantu orang itu untuk menanam banyak pepohonan di kota.

17

They plant grass and flowering bushes and lots and lots of trees including fruit trees too. Other people who live in the city help too. Everyone said that the city looks much better now!

Mereka menanam rumput dan semak-semak berbunga dan banyak pepohonan termasuk pohon buah- buahan. Orang lain yang hidup di kota juga membantu. Setiap orang menyatakan bahwa kota itu nampak jauh lebih baik sekarang!

18

Tree returns home. Tree is glad to be back in the country where there are lots of plants.

Pohon pulang kembali ke rumah. Pohon merasa senang bisa kembali ke pedesaan yang banyak pepohonan.

19

Suddenly, tree sees a plane high up in the sky.

Tiba- tiba, pohon melihat sebuah
pesawat terbang tinggi di angkasa.

20

Tree thinks, "I wonder where the plane is going? Next harvest, I will go on another trip! There are more places to visit! The world is a wide wonderful place!"

Pohon berpikir, "Aku bertanya-tanya ke mana pesawat itu akan pergi?" Musim panen berikutnya, aku akan pergi ke perjalanan berikutnya! Ada banyak tempat untuk dikunjungi! Dunia merupakan satu tempat indah yang luas!"

21

ALFORD e-Books

available on:
Google Play

Printed Books

available at:
www.createspace.com
www.amazon.com

Please contact us at:
alfordbooks1story@gmail.com
or trythaiketco@gmail.com

www.ALFORDebooks.com

All About England!

Douglas J. and Pakaket Alford

23

"Free English eBooks from Alford Books"

Google Drive:
https://drive.google.com/folderview?id=0B9EO9Ya
GIIwPcDBrNzhvZkc1WVk&usp=sharing

or Dropbox
https://www.dropbox.com/sh/dyjj4a5orfynwg5/
AAAQCF15TZXXGMvYHnV5WQUNa?dl=0

Free Alford e-Books available on Google Play!

See Free Alford Video-Books on YouTube
https://www.youtube.com/channel/
UCk0hH52xaTRQgC4GVB2oI9A

PRINTED BOOK Available at: www.amazon.com

24

25

Monkey Star

Bee's Sneeze

Money Math

Hedgehogs Hug!

Too Much TV

Jungle Fire!

All About England!

Sand Sea
-Full of Desert Life

Ogs, Zogs and
Useful Cogs
- A Tale of Teamwork

Chase
to Space
The Space Race Story

Life Then
- Applies Today

Big Die
- Earth's Mass Extinctions

Computers
Are Easy to Understand

Civil
Sense
What if there wasn't a Civil War?

Sky-Lings:
An Intro to Airplanes

Art Intro -
With Insects,
Eggs and Oils

Nature's
Links of Life

Computer Come-Froms
The Roots of Real-Time

www.ALFORDebooks.com

English ABC

- Alford Book Club

Lessons 1 to 7

Douglas J. & Pakaket Alford

26

Teacher
Instruction Guide

Panduan Mengajar untuk Guru

Indonesian
A5

English
ABC
- Alford
Book
Club

Lessons 1 to 7

27

Douglas J. & Pakaket Alford
Translated by Sri Harto

46120620R00019

Made in the USA
Middletown, DE
23 July 2017